The Insider's Guide to New Orleans

The Insider's Guides

The Insider's Guide to New Orleans
Honey Naylor

The Insider's Guide to San Diego
James B. Kelleher

The Insider's Guide to Santa Fe, Third Edition
Bill Jamison and Cheryl Alters Jamison

The Insider's Guide
to
NEW ORLEANS

Honey Naylor

THE HARVARD COMMON PRESS
Boston, Massachusetts

For M & D

♦ ♦ ♦ ♦ ♦ ♦ ♦

The Harvard Common Press
535 Albany Street
Boston, Massachusetts 02118

Printed in the United States of America

LIBRARY OF CONGRESS CATALOGING-IN-PUBLICATION DATA

Naylor, Honey.
   The insider's guide to New Orleans / Honey Naylor.
      p.   cm. — (The Insider's guides)
   Includes index.
   ISBN 1-55832-063-6
      1. New Orleans (La.)—Guidebooks.   I. Title.   II. Series:
   Insider's guides (Boston, Mass.)
   F379.N53N4   1994
   917.63'350463-dc20   93-41742
                                                                  CIP

Maps by Charles Bahne
Cover design by Jackie Schuman

10   9   8   7   6   5   4   3   2   1

Contents

Maps

Acknowledgments
◆◆◆◆◆◆◆◆◆◆◆◆◆◆◆◆

F irst, my sincerest gratitude to Beverly Gianna, Public Relations Director for the Greater New Orleans Tourist and Convention Commission. Beverly and her staff know all there is to know about the city and share their knowledge with generosity and good cheer. My thanks to all of them.

To Jessica Travis and Pamela Arceneaux at the Historic New Orleans Collection, my undying gratitude! They came to my aid any number of times, and I am most appreciative.

Thanks, too, to Bruce Morgan, Director of Communications at the Louisiana State Office of Tourism. Bruce is a walking encyclopedia of Louisiana-ana who knows every nook and cranny in the state. I'm indebted to him not only for his invaluable help but for his patience all of those times I called him when my hair was on fire and I needed instant assistance. Thanks a million.

A special word of thanks to Carola Ann Andrepont in Opelousas, who is a great asset to the state. The people of Louisiana are the greatest in the world (say I, a native of the state), and my job was made much easier by their friendliness and generosity.

I'm indebted to my editor, Leslie Baker, a woman with a keen eye and fine sense of humor. She kept me from going off on numerous tangents and writing a book about three times the size it should be, and she did so with tact and wit.

For years my friend Claudia Miller urged me to write. I insisted I couldn't; she insisted I could. Finally I stopped arguing and began writing. I am much obliged to her for her faith and persistence.

I'd also like to add a word of thanks to South Louisiana music. In writing about this state, I am required to eat tons of the world's best food. Happily, the intoxicating, syncopating, and utterly irresistible rhythms of Cajun and zydeco bands have kept my feet flying and my weight down.

On a very personal note, I'd like to express my gratitude to my parents, the late Charles and Heroise Warren Naylor, for their genes, support, and belief in me. They are the M & D—Mama and Daddy, as we Southerners say—to whom this book is dedicated.

Introduction
♦♦♦♦♦♦♦♦♦♦♦
A Celebration of the Senses

F RANCIS FORD COPPOLA has a house in the
French Quarter just down the street from fellow
director Taylor Hackford's. Actor John Goodman is seen
around town so often that most locals assume he lives
here. New Orleans is where Julia Roberts and Denzel
Washington filed *The Pelican Brief*; where Kevin Costner
and company shot scenes for *JFK*; where Dennis Quaid
romanced Ellen Barkin in *The Big Easy*; where Paul
Newman portrayed Louisiana governor Earl Long in pur-
suit of *Blaze*; and where even the debonair James Bond
(Roger Moore) put in an appearance in *Live and Let Die*.
The Crescent City was a most appropriate setting when
Tom Cruise assumed the role of Vampire Lestat in the
film version of homegrown writer Anne Rice's best seller
Interview with the Vampire. And many an Orleanian
remembers when Elia Kazan directed Vivien Leigh and a
host of local extras in the opening scenes of *A Streetcar
Named Desire*, when Blanche arrives at Union Station.

Small wonder that so many people in the film industry
turn up in New Orleans to work and to play: The city's

French Quarter just *looks* like a movie set; as if some flamboyant set designer with French and Spanish blood flowing in his veins and visions of Oscars dancing in his head had been turned loose. New Orleans is one of the best places in the world for dreaming dreams, and there are worlds of places here for daydreaming. The Napoleon House is a favorite local lazing place, as is Lafitte's Blacksmith Shop—both are watering holes and but two among dozens of atmospheric saloons.

But long before the movie and TV people came pouring in, the French Quarter—the original city that the Creoles founded—was a haven for other artists. In the 1820s John James Audubon worked in Louisiana, creating eighty of his Birds of America masterpieces in New Orleans and in the Feliciana parishes (counties) north of Baton Rouge.

In 1796 the nation's oldest opera association was founded in New Orleans; throughout the nineteenth century, opera was performed here on a grand scale. Jenny Lind (the "Swedish Nightingale") sang here in 1851, courtesy of impresario P. T. Barnum; and the young Adelina Patti, another nineteenth century songbird of considerable notes, thrilled the throngs in the French Opera House on Bourbon Street.

But the city is much better known for another kind of music: jazz. Many famed New Orleans musicians of the latter part of the nineteenth century played ragtime and rinky-dink piano in the "sporting houses" of Storyville, the city's notorious red-light district. Storyville, a civic effort to contain rampant prostitution within strictly enforced boundaries, flourished from 1897 until 1917 when the U. S. Navy shut it down. *Jazz* is a sanitized version of the word *jass* (a term bandied about in Storyville's houses of ill repute), which had less to do with music than with the goings on within the houses. Storyville is long gone, but its music continues to go through the roofs of dingy dives, sleek clubs, and even frilly riverboats.

Louis Armstrong was a native son. Jelly Roll Morton lived here, and Fats Domino still does. This is the hometown of the Neville Brothers, Wynton and Branford Marsalis, Pete Fountain, Harry Connick, Jr., Al Hirt, and Allen Toussaint, whose numerous compositions include the sultry "Southern Nights." Ellis Marsalis, father of Wynton, Branford, and talented young Delfeayo, is highly regarded in New Orleans, where he is both professor of music and performer.

The Crescent City has long been an inspiration for writers. Mark Twain was nuts about New Orleans; his *Life on the Mississippi* devotes ten chapters to his irrepressible impressions. Actually, Twain was Samuel Clemens until he adopted his pen name while writing for the *New Orleans Crescent*—a paper that had earlier employed Walt Whitman. While working here in 1848, Whitman wrote "I Saw in Louisiana a Live Oak Growing." Another famous pen name was adopted in New Orleans when William Sidney Porter became O. Henry over drinks in a local bar.

In the twenties and thirties the French Quarter was to New Orleans what the Left Bank was to Paris—a haven for artists and writers. Gertrude Stein, John Dos Passos, Sherwood Anderson, and William Faulkner were among those who wandered in and out. Faulkner wrote his first novel in an apartment overlooking romantic Pirate's Alley. In the forties, the rumble of the streetcars rolling along Royal Street inspired Tennessee Williams to write his Pulitzer Prize–winning *A Streetcar Named Desire*. In 1980 a Pulitzer was awarded posthumously to John Kennedy Toole for *A Confederacy of Dunces*; despite Toole's tragic suicide, it is a wildly funny book that perfectly captures New Orleans' distinctive dialects and rich flavor —a must-read for anyone planning a visit.

The French Quarter is a small town within the city. It covers about a square mile and has fewer than five thousand residents, many of whom rarely venture beyond its borders. Neighbors on the way to the Royal Street A&P or Galatoire's or Harry's Place stop on the street to chat and smile at strangers in passing. There are neighborhood crime watches, civic organizations, schools, dentists, and drugstores—in all of these respects the Quarter is a small town. But it is highly unlikely that there is any other small town like it. As in most small towns, every Quarterite knows every other one's business; the difference here is that Quarter denizens cut each other a lot of slack. That may well be one of the reasons that celebrities keep buying up real estate here; like any other locals—Ruthie the Duck Lady or the Bead Lady or Chicken Man—they're left alone to do as they please.

New Orleans is a good-time town with a Latinesque emphasis on the sensuous. Festivals seem to crop up out of every crack in the flagstones. The best chefs in town are celebrities of superstar magnitude. New Orleanians adore their music, food, festivals, and fun. This may very well be a result of the city's desperate origins: It's the Big Easy now, but in the eighteenth century it was just a big mess. Read on . . .

PART ONE

◆◆◆◆◆◆◆◆◆◆◆

THE FRENCH CONNECTION

Chapter One
♦♦♦♦♦♦♦♦♦♦♦
The Trembling Earth

MUCH FICTION has been written in and about New Orleans, but the true story of the city is as unlikely a tale as any that a scenarist might devise. The cast includes several kings and scores of criminals; presidents and dashing pirates; swashbuckling explorers, soldiers of fortune, and indigenous Indians; feisty priests, saintly nuns, and scarifying voodoo queens; and a whole raft of gamblers and sundry villains with nefarious schemes.

Key players in the melodrama that evolved into New Orleans were a motley group of settlers made up largely of miscellaneous misfits, recalcitrant criminals, and unreformed prostitutes, all of whom were sent forth to establish a French foothold smack in the midst of squishy swamps.

La terre tremblante, the earliest French settlers called this place: the trembling earth. About a hundred years later, around the turn of the nineteenth century, Napoleon Bonaparte, whose calculating eye was fixed on what had by then become a strategic port, dubbed it the Isle d'Orléans.

Although it lies well inland—the Gulf of Mexico laps at the ragged coastline about 110 miles to the south— New Orleans is still an island, wrapped in waterways and sunk in a bowl about five feet below sea level. Although it lies on a line with Cairo and Shanghai, in temperament and tempo it has much in common with its cousins in the Caribbean. Subtropical and sultry, it is decorated with pale green banana plants, tall palms, sweet olive, jasmine, and bougainvillea. Like all of South Louisiana, the city is festooned with giant live oak trees dressed to the nines in long gray trains of Spanish moss. To qualify for membership in the Louisiana Live Oak Society, founded in 1934, you must be at least a hundred years old, and a tree.

Instead of being fringed with white sand beaches, this inland island is surrounded by marshlands, bayous, and swamps. The marshes appear to be fields of tall waving green grass. But if you strike out across them, as the French probably did, you'll sink right down into the trembling earth. And it isn't earth at all, but still water. Lakes, too, dot the area around the island: Maurepas, Borgne, and St. Catherine, as well as the nation's seventh-largest, Lake Pontchartrain, which forms a forty-mile shallow water border north of New Orleans. The lake is twenty-four miles wide and it was not until 1957 that a causeway (the world's longest) was built across it, thereby connecting New Orleans with St. Tammany Parish on the lake's north shore. And as late as 1958, the Greater Mississippi Bridge, now called the Crescent City Connection, was built to hook downtown New Orleans to the West Bank—which lies due east of the East Bank. In New Orleans the sun comes up over the West Bank, much of which is south of the city. That's because of the mightiest, and most romantic, of all the waterways that caress the Crescent City.

The mighty Mississippi divides New Orleans the way the Seine splits Paris. The Mississippi is much more contorted than the Seine, however, and because of its various twists, Orleanians long ago dispensed with ordinary compass points. Here there is no North, South, East, or West; locals simply go with the flow: Uptown is upriver, downtown is downriver, lakeside is toward Lake Pontchartrain, and riverside is toward the cause of all this confusion. It takes you a while to figure out exactly where to go when you're told, "I'll meet you on the downtown riverside corner."

Old Man River has the lead role in the story of New Orleans. He wears a million masks and is as unpredictable and fickle a river as nature ever formed. The inspiration for lyricists and poets, he can lull you into the most romantic of moods, then suddenly turn mean as murder and scare the living daylights out of you. The U. S. Army Corps of Engineers dams him and valiantly tries to contain him, but the river strains to be released, to follow his natural instincts. For some time now he has been itching to switch off toward the 800,000-acre Atchafalaya Basin over to the west in Louisiana's Cajun Country; the Atchafalaya is part of the vast system of spillways that slurp up excess waters and soak up silt when the Mississippi goes on a rampage. The tremendous loads of silt being deposited in northern Atchafalaya Bay are gradually, but very surely, forming a new land mass. People who study these things predict that by 2020 a new delta, covering 192,000 acres, will extend south of Morgan City, beyond Point au Fer Island in the Gulf of Mexico.

The Corps of Engineers knows what's on the Old Man's mind and is well aware of the havoc he could wreak by going his own way. If he changes his course, the grand and glorious show that is New Orleans will probably close and the scene could conceivably shift to a floating land called Isle d'Atchafalaya. The Mississippi is at once New Orleans' *raison d'être* and its *bête noire*. For many centuries the temperamental river has been the producer, director, set designer, and star of the show—a showboater if ever there was one. Were it not for Old Man River, there would be no tale to tell.

The Mississippi begins as a small stream flowing out of Lake Itasca in northern Minnesota; at the river's source, you can easily straddle it. It snakes southward 2,350 miles through the heartland of North America, widens to a mile and a half at the point where various tributaries churn in, and then narrows somewhat before emptying into the Gulf of Mexico through a vast, fan-shaped delta in Louisiana. The land in Louisiana, and the alluvial plain, are new, at least in terms of eternity. The northern portion of the river counts its years in the millions; Louisiana's shoreline is a mere child of some six thousand years, shaped by the interaction of the gulf's waters and the river's sediments. The coastal marshes are studded with "islands" that are actually salt domes covered with lush vegetation. It is the newness of the coastline that causes geologists to keep a weather eye on the delta shaping up in the Atchafalaya Bay.

Three hundred rivers flow into the Mississippi river system, with waters from as far east as New York State and as far west as Montana extending the length of the river to almost thirty-five hundred miles. It is North America's longest river and the world's third longest; only the Nile and the Amazon are greater in length. Meandering through its great basin, the river drains 41 percent of the United States and three Canadian provinces for a total of 1,245 million square miles. It is indeed a great river.

The Indians encountered by the first European explorers were well acquainted with the Mississippi. To the

Algonquins in the far north all the way down to the Pascagoula near the Gulf of Mexico, the river was a main highway; smaller rivers, streams, and bayous were but country roads for the first inhabitants. (The Mississippi was I-95 without the traffic.) The great river has traveled under many aliases—Spanish, French, and Indian. The first Spaniards who saw this mighty body of water called it, variously, Rio Grande, Rio del Espirito Santo, and Palizada—the last because of the palisades-like mud formations at the river's mouth. One of several French names given the river was St. Louis, in honor of the seemingly indestructible Sun King. There were any number of Indian names for the river; *Mississippi* is probably Algonquian, roughly translating to "Father of Waters."

Indians roamed the lower Mississippi valley for at least twelve thousand years before European contact. There are several important archaeological sites in the state. Some of the mounds found in Louisiana date to 4000 B.C. and are among the oldest in North America. The two mounds on the campus of Louisiana State University in Baton Rouge date to 3000 B.C. One of the nation's most important archaeological sites, dating to 1200 B.C., is Poverty Point in northeast Louisiana. The largest mound there is seven stories high—an enormous piece of work considering the dearth of bulldozers at the time. The digs at Poverty Point are of particular interest because excavated evidence indicates a great deal of movement among early peoples. Poverty Point seems to have been a major trading center for the entire Mississippi valley; material unearthed there was traded from as far away as the Great Lakes and the Appalachians. It is hypothesized that the Marksville people, who came to this area from the Ohio valley, probably drove away the Poverty Point people. Both the Poverty Point site and the Marksville site, the latter in South Louisiana, are open to the public.

By the seventeenth century, when the French first arrived, there were about fifteen thousand Indian inhabitants in the lower Mississippi valley, including the Natchez, Pascagoula, Tunica, Tensas, Choctaw, Caddo, and Chickasaw. But prior to the French there were the Spaniards. Although almost nothing is known about the Indians who were encountered by the Spanish explorers, there is certainly no doubt about their presence.

In 1539 an expeditionary party led by Hernando de Soto landed near present-day Tampa Bay and began nosing around for gold. Alternately abducting and decimating Indians as they moved north and westward, the Spaniards finally did indeed find a treasure: the mighty Mississippi, which they happened upon on May 21, 1541. De Soto probably claimed everything in sight for Spain, but it was a claim in vain; in less than a year, on a riverbank in Louisiana, de Soto died of a fever. His fellow explorers buried him in the Big Muddy so that the Indians, whose feelings toward him were less than charitable, would not know of his death.

De Soto's claim on the Louisiana Territory was on the order of whistling Dixie, and it was more than 140 years before anyone made a claim that stuck. In the late seventeenth century, a Frenchman by the name of René-Robert Cavelier, Sieur de La Salle, swashed and buckled his way by canoe from the juncture of the Illinois and Mississippi rivers down to the mouth of the Big Muddy. Accompanying him was a group that included his friend and ally Henri de Tonti, an Italian soldier of fortune. At the Gulf of Mexico, on April 9, 1682, La Salle proclaimed that all of the territory drained by the Mississippi belonged to France. No doubt with appropriate Gallic flair—and the French fleur-de-lis unfurled—he christened the land Louisiane in honor of Louis XIV, the Sun King, and plunged a tall, sturdy wooden cross into the moist earth to mark the spot.

At that particular time Louis had his hands full persecuting Huguenots, pursuing sundry mistresses, and moving his entire court to the newly completed Versailles. He had neither the time nor the inclination to fool with some sodden, worthless chunk of real estate halfway around the world. However, some of his ministers were interested, and La Salle obtained permission—though nothing in the way of funding—to return to the New World and set up house.

Notwithstanding the cross and the staked-out claim, La Salle was unable to carry out his plans for a colony at the mouth of the Mississippi. Perhaps his navigational skills got a bit rusty during the five years he spent conferring with finance ministers. Whatever the case, La Salle was unable to find Louisiane. In 1687 he was murdered by his own men when he tried to make his way up to Canada—a rather harsh punishment for someone who'd simply lost his way.

La Salle and de Tonti, who sailed downriver from Illinois, had planned to rendezvous at an Indian camp between Baton Rouge and New Orleans. When de Tonti failed to locate La Salle or learn anything of his whereabouts, he left a letter for La Salle with a chief of the Bayougoulas. The chief must have sensed the letter's importance: He kept it for more than twelve years, and presented it to the French explorers who came later.

La Salle is properly credited with establishing the French foothold in Louisiana and claiming and naming the territory for the Sun King. But the man recognized as the founder of Louisiana was thirty-seven-year-old Pierre Le Moyne, Sieur d'Iberville—a war hero and a French Creole.

Chapter Two

The Mississippi Bubble

I N THE mid-sixteenth century, about the time Hernando de Soto was headed for the Florida shore, the
French began establishing a presence in Canada. In 1534
Jacques Cartier, a French seaman, sailed into the Gulf of
St. Lawrence and claimed New France for Francis I. In
1603 Samuel de Champlain sailed into the Bay of Fundy
and founded in present-day Nova Scotia the first French
colony in North America. The original settlers, the Mic-
mac Indians, had called the area Acadia, and that was the
name adopted by the French. (The Acadian settlers turned
out to be highly significant in the development of Louisiana.) Five years later, in 1608, Quebec was established—
at the same time the first English settlers in the New
World were struggling to survive in Jamestown, Virginia.
Just as the English settlers were the actors in the drama
unfolding on the Atlantic Seaboard, so would the French
Canadians play major roles in the development of early
Louisiana.

Pierre Le Moyne, Sieur d'Iberville, and his brother
Jean-Baptiste Le Moyne, Sieur de Bienville—respectively,

the founder of Louisiana and the founder of New Orleans—were two of the eleven sons of a fur trader who had emigrated from Normandy to Montreal. (*Sieur* roughly translates to "lord," a title conferred upon a commoner by the Crown.) In the waning years of the seventeenth century Iberville had distinguished himself in the Hudson Bay campaign of King William's War, and he was a celebrated naval war hero. In 1699 Louis XIV bestirred himself to dispatch Iberville, with an expeditionary force that included Bienville, soldiers, and about two hundred settlers, to follow through on La Salle's earlier claims to territory on the Gulf of Mexico.

Iberville and his band set up camps or forts in what are now Biloxi, Mississippi, and Mobile and Dauphine Island, Alabama, and set off to explore the Mississippi. The earliest seats of French colonial government on the Gulf Coast were at Biloxi and Mobile; in the early eighteenth century, Dauphine Island on Mobile Bay was the Ellis Island of the Louisiana Territory.

With Choctaw guides the Frenchmen traveled north of what the Indians called Okwata ("wide water"). Although Iberville may have thought the name pretty, and certainly appropriate, he rechristened the large lake Pontchartrain in honor of Louis XIV's minister of the marine, and he named a nearby, smaller lake Maurepas after Pontchartrain's son. A bit farther north the explorers spied a red stick that Indians had plunged into a bluff above the river. Iberville noted it in his diary as "Baton Rouge," and the town later established on that site became the present-day capital of Louisiana.

When Iberville sailed for France to obtain more settlers and supplies, Bienville, who had been commissioned as commandant, or acting governor, stayed in Louisiana and continued to explore. The Indians had shown him and his brother an overland portage that connected a *bayuk*—the Indian word for bayou—with the Mississippi, and

Bienville named it Bayou St. John for his patron saint. Nowadays that area is Mid-City, a sprawling residential district, but in the early eighteenth century it was a sprawling swamp, a residential district of snakes, alligators, and mosquitos. The scattered homes in these swamplands were built on natural levees, or "ridges," to give them a leg up out of the frequent floods. One of the outstanding stars of early Louisiana history had a concession in that area: Louis Juchereau de St. Denis, who founded the town of Natchitoches in north-central Louisiana in 1714, four years before the founding of New Orleans. Natchitoches is the oldest permanent European settlement in the Louisiana Territory.

Iberville died in 1706 (on the eve of a major expedition he was to lead against the British in the War of Spanish Succession), and Bienville became acting governor of the Louisiana Territory. Six years later a wealthy Parisian named Antoine Crozat was granted a fifteen-year royal charter to operate the Louisiana Territory. Crozat dismissed Bienville and named as governor the man who had founded Detroit at the turn of the century: Antoine de Lamothe Cadillac, a fellow who apparently alienated everyone with whom he came in contact. (He especially riled the Indians.) Within five years, a disgusted Crozat saw that his venture was a total disaster and asked to be relieved of his responsibility. Bienville continued to hunker down in Louisiana: His day was coming.

In New Orleans no monuments, historic sites, statues, or plaques pay tribute to the man who was really responsible for getting the city on the map: John Law. Law is almost totally ignored because, his name notwithstanding, the man was a crook. He was, however, something of a trendsetter. Louisiana has a long and colorful history of political shenanigans; perhaps it's in the state's genes, courtesy of Law's cunning.

A Scot who fled England after killing a man in a duel,

Law gambled throughout Europe before finally oiling his way into the glittering, glamorous, and totally degenerate French court of the Bourbons. Thanks to his friendship with the schemer Philippe II, duc d'Orléans, who was young Louis XV's regent, Law obtained a twenty-five-year charter to exploit the Louisiana Territory. After handpicking Bienville to be its governor, he embarked on an ambitious and complicated scheme that came to be called the Mississippi Bubble.

The extravagances of the court of Louis XIV had left France with an enormous debt. According to Law's philosophy, the debt should be paid off not by the French Crown but by the French public. In 1716 he established the Banque Générale, a bank that had the authority to issue notes, and a year later he organized the Company of the West, later known as the Company of the Indies. In short order the bank and the company merged, and Law finagled complete control over all of France's colonial trade and finances, including the minting of French money and the collecting of French taxes. Law sold his company's shares to the public in exchange for state-issued public securities. With people scrambling to buy up shares, a veritable feeding frenzy ensued and the price per share shot skyward—far out of proportion to the company's earnings. The French government exploited the general stock market boom that was spreading through Europe by printing paper money, which France's creditors accepted and used to buy more shares in the Company of the Indies. Yet more paper money was printed. The result was runaway inflation and ultimately a crash that thundered throughout Europe. By 1720 the bubble had burst, France and sundry other European countries had gone belly up, and Law had departed in disgrace.

In addition to relieving people of their money, Law had instructed Bienville to establish a settlement in the Louisiana Territory and to call it la Nouvelle Orléans after his friend the regent. In 1717 Bienville selected what he thought would be the ideal site: on the high ground at a great bend in the Mississippi. It was on a crescent-shaped bend, no less, and *voila!*—we have the Crescent City.

Progress was hampered by the state's wildness as well as by world class hurricanes that quickly swept away the first primitive shacks. The sight of crude shelters of palmetto and bark must have struck horror in the hearts of the next wave of immigrants—a surly, hard-bitten group of criminals and prostitutes who preferred imprisonment over banishment to the wild unknown. But Philippe and company saw the colony—which, after all, needed colonists—as a fine way to clear out overcrowded French prisons and sweep the miscreants off of the French streets. By 1720 the first group of slaves had arrived. In 1721 la Nouvelle Orléans and its environs had a population of almost 1,750, including slaves.

The city's design, laid out by Adrien de Pauger according to the plans of royal engineer Pierre Le Blond de La Tour, followed that of a medieval village in France: At the town's center was the main square, Place d'Armes, the hub of all social, religious, and governmental activities. Later, during the Spanish colonial period, it was Plaza de Armas. To the Americans it was the Public Square, and still later, Jackson Square, the name by which it is now known.

In 1727 the first Ursuline nuns arrived in the colony. The twelve Sisters of St. Ursula survived a turbulent, terrifying five-month voyage from Rouen before reaching what one of them described, charitably, as a cesspool. Today's Old Ursuline Convent on Chartres Street in the French Quarter, on the site of their original convent, was completed in 1745. Of major national importance, this building is the only undisputed survivor of the conflagrations that swept through la Nouvelle Orléans in the late eighteenth century. It is the only extant structure that dates to Bienville's original colony, and it is the oldest building in the lower Mississippi valley.

Before the arrival of the sisters, however, Bienville had been complaining to the Crown about the quality of the folks who were being sent to populate the city. In addition to the hardships that Mother Nature was throwing his way, Bienville was being sent the sort of people who made him fear for his very life. His complaints finally got results. The same year that the Ursulines came to la Nouvelle Orléans, the government sent to the colony a group of marriageable young ladies of good stock to help stabilize the settlement. (The French government had provided each of the ladies with small chests packed with clothing and personal effects. Because these chests were known as *cassettes* in French, their bearers later came to be known as the Casket Girls.) But the biggest boost in the city's development was the arrival of the German settlers in the early 1720s. The two thousand who actually made it over (ten thousand were recruited) settled upriver on what became known as the German Coast, and to the southwest, where their descendants still live in the place called Des Allemands. The sturdy, hard-working German farmers provided much-needed stability for the new colony.

In 1723 the capital was moved from Mobile to la Nouvelle Orléans largely due to Bienville's agitations toward that goal. But despite the best efforts of Bienville, the tender mercies of the Ursulines, and the hard work of the Germans, la Nouvelle Orléans did not fare well. In 1724, while Bienville was away in France, the bloody Natchez Massacre took place upriver—an event that was precipitated by the arrival of the French commandant at Fort Rosalie. Provoked by the commandant, the Natchez slaughtered some three hundred French settlers; in retaliation the French basically annihilated the Natchez Indian nation. The debacle, and the costs incurred, caused the Company of the Indies, which was still operating the Louisiana Territory, to petition the French Crown to relieve it of its responsibilities. Thus in 1731 Louisiana reverted to the French court and became a crown colony. At the time, it had a population of only seven thousand— five thousand white settlers and two thousand African slaves. The following year, Bienville returned to Louisiana for his last term as governor, serving for another twelve years before requesting that he be allowed to retire and return to France.

During the entire period when France was trying, how- ever listlessly, to finance, populate, and control the Loui- siana Territory, she was engaged in the seventy-four-year French and Indian Wars (1689–1763). Somewhat mis- named by American historians, the French and Indian Wars were battles fought between the French and the British over colonial holdings extending all the way from Canada down to the Caribbean. The campaigns, which could be characterized as one long war with intermittent coffee breaks, were intertwined with a series of world- wide territorial wars that involved Spain and Austria as well as France and England—not to mention Thirteen Colonies that were a-borning on the Eastern Seaboard.

As the conflicts drew to a close, it seemed likely that peace negotiations would result in Spain's loss of her Florida colonies to England. In 1763, by the secret Treaty of Fontainebleau, Bourbon France ceded Louisiana to Bourbon Spain. (It is probably untrue that Louis XV lost a bet with his cousin, King Charles III of Spain, and paid off his debt with the entire Louisiana Territory; more likely France aimed to keep Louisiana "all in the family" —and to get rid of what had been a great financial drain.)

The year 1762 also saw the arrival of the first Acadians to Louisiana. A few years before France and Spain signed the Fontainebleau treaty, the Acadians, descendants of the

French colonists who had arrived in New France at the dawn of the seventeenth century, were exiled by the British from their homes in what is now Nova Scotia. When New France came under English rule, the British expelled the Acadians from their homes. Between five and ten thousand of them eventually came to Louisiana and settled in the parishes to the west of New Orleans—the area called, variously, Cajun Country, Acadiana, and French Louisiana.

The general worldwide hostilities came to an end in 1763 with the signing of the Treaty of Paris, under which France lost all of her North American colonies, including Canada, and all of the land south of the Great Lakes and east of the Mississippi. All French territories east of the Mississippi were ceded to England except for the Isle d'Orléans, which, with the rest of Louisiana, had already become the property of Spain. But the governor of the colony, Jean-Jacques Blaise d'Abbadie, was not notified of the transfer until 1764 (he died shortly thereafter). When the citizenry of la Nouvelle Orléans, accustomed to doing pretty much as they pleased under the lax French rule, were apprised that they'd been acquired by Spain, they flatly refused to accept it, and life continued on as it had before. Even before the new governor, Don Antonio de Ulloa, finally showed up in March 1766 with fewer than a hundred soldiers, a group of local merchants had begun to conspire against the Spaniards. By October hundreds of Orleanians, joined by Germans and Acadians, were rioting in the streets. At the behest of the colony's superior council, Ulloa sailed off into the sunset.

For some Louisianians, this insurrection, coming as it did six years before the revolt of the Thirteen Colonies, represented the first American Revolution against foreign rule. If so, it was a mighty brave—or suicidal—group of revolutionaries. At the time of the Spanish occupation, about three thousand people lived in la Nouvelle Orléans;

the colony as a whole had a population of about thirteen thousand five hundred. By most accounts, this demonstration more closely resembled a temper tantrum than a revolution.

In 1769 change did come for the city in the person of General Alejandro O'Reilly, an Irishman in the service of Spain. O'Reilly and his fleet of twenty-four warships and twenty-six hundred troops saw to it that la Nouvelle Orléans was born again as Nueva Orleans. During his seven months in Louisiana, O'Reilly punished the instigators of the riot that had ousted Ulloa, substituted Spanish law and Spanish currency for French, disbanded the Superior Council, and set in motion plans for a building to house the Spanish *cabildo*, or town council. Louisiana's designation of "parishes" as political districts rather than counties dates from O'Reilly's subdivision of the colony into parishes of the Catholic Church.

Louisiana, a drain on the French coffers, continued to be costly for Spain, too. But under the Spanish, who were better administrators than the French, Louisiana began to flourish. More and more immigrants arrived, agriculture really got off the ground, and the strategically located port of la Nouvelle Orléans achieved major importance. In the 1790s the Spanish governor Francisco Luis Hector, Baron de Carondelet, strengthened the city's fortifications and established the first theater, newspaper, and police department. He also constructed the Carondelet Canal (also known as the Old Basin Canal), which connected the French Quarter with Lake Pontchartrain via Bayou St. John. But despite the presence of Spanish administrators, law, and currency, Louisiana never did become a Spanish colony. Apart from some isolated cases, during Spain's four decades of governance the only Spaniards who moved to Louisiana were government administrators.

Two cataclysmic fires in the late eighteenth century destroyed most of Bienville's original colony. The rebuilt city was, and is, decidedly Spanish in character. The French, too, left indelible marks on the Louisiana Territory. The French language and customs were adopted, at least to some degree, by Germans, by African slaves, and later by immigrants to the colony. The French colonial period also left its approach to governing, a style that roughly corresponds to an elaborate Gallic shrug.

At the turn of the nineteenth century, France again turned an interested eye on Louisiana when la Nouvelle Orléans' strategically located port attracted the roving eye of Napoleon Bonaparte. In 1800 the Little Corporal persuaded Spain to retrocede the Louisiana Territory to France—and, as before, the transfer was by secret treaty. Thomas Jefferson, who was elected president of the still young United States in 1800, neither liked nor trusted Napoleon—with some justification, considering the Corsican's penchant for devouring countries. Jefferson had no intention of losing the valuable port of la Nouvelle Orléans to the French dictator, and he sent Robert Livingston and James Monroe to Paris to negotiate the purchase of the Isle d'Orléans from Bonaparte. Napoleon, who had attempted to take control of Louisiana from a headquarters set up in French-held Santo Domingo, was thwarted both by the slave revolt that erupted there in the 1790s and by a yellow fever epidemic. He decided to sell not just the Isle d'Orléans but the entire Louisiana Territory to Jefferson for $15 million—not a bad deal considering that the real estate included all of the territory from the Mississippi to the Rockies and from the Gulf of Mexico to British North America. The historic Louisiana Purchase, then, was a steal at four cents an acre.

Chapter Three
♦♦♦♦♦♦♦♦♦♦♦♦♦

The Creoles and the Americans

EVER SINCE it was laid out in 1721, Jackson Square has been scene of sundry activities—from lashings and hangings to festivals and Christmas caroling. In 1803 it served as the backdrop for two highly significant ceremonies within a three-week period. On November 30, Pierre de Laussat, representing France, accepted Louisiana from Spain. (The ceremony was merely a formality; the territory had already been transferred three years earlier.) Then, on December 20, the French flag was lowered in the public square and the American flag was raised, and la Nouvelle Orléans became New Orleans.

New Orleans had come a long way from her rough-and-tumble origins. Reared as a waterfront brat, she had matured considerably over the years and taken on a somewhat more sophisticated air (which is not to say she was an educated lady. Historical inventories of early creole homes have unearthed few books but plenty of gambling paraphernalia. New Orleanians were also fond of dancing, parties, the theater, and opera). Above all, she was extremely proud of her French Creole heritage.

The word *creole* is greatly misunderstood, and it is used incorrectly more often than not. It is an Anglicized version of the Spanish word *crillo*, which was originally used to distinguish a thoroughbred Spanish child born in the Spanish colonies from a child of a mixed marriage. These days virtually anything indigenous to the New Orleans area is labeled "creole." When used as an adjective, the word is spelled with a small *c*, and as a noun it is spelled with a capital: There is creole architecture, creole cuisine, creole yams and tomatoes, creole music, and, of course, Creoles (the people).

Under the social code of the day, Creole gentlemen did not necessarily pursue such activities as, say, work. Although indolence was not frowned upon, certain kinds of occupations were. A Creole could be a planter, a physician, a lawyer—a professional man. He was always dapper. He spent his days lolling about coffeehouses, or gambling, or dueling. All of the "better" people seem to have done a great deal of dueling, having honed their skills at the fencing masters' academies in Exchange Alley. Favored fighting places were in St. Anthony's Garden behind St. Louis Cathedral or beneath the Dueling Oaks in City Park. The challenge, *Allons sous les chênes*! ("Let's go under the oaks"), was the Creole equivalent of "Let's step outside." Many a duel was fought over a sloe-eyed quadroon beauty with skin the color of *café au lait*.

Scores of refugees poured into the city from Santo Domingo after the slave revolt of 1791. Many white *and* black slaveholders brought with them their slaves and as many of their household possessions as they could manage. Mulattoes and quadroons (people who are one-quarter black) were *gens de couleur libres* ("free people of color") who came to the Crescent City. Which brings up the quadroon balls: the means by which mulatto mothers introduced their quadroon daughters to Creole gentlemen for the purpose of making an "alliance." The balls were lavish affairs "produced" by entrepreneurs and held in locations all over the city. Wearing white shawls and with their heads wrapped in *tignons* (turbans), mothers escorted their elegantly attired daughters and kept a watchful eye on the dancing and the flirting. If a man expressed interest in a particular young girl, he and her mother hammered out an agreement detailing the exact financial arrangements of the alliance.

All of the above was part of the system called *plaçage*, which, along with other French customs, had crossed the Atlantic and settled in New Orleans. In plain English it meant that many wealthy young Creoles took mistresses —usually free women of color—with whom they lived in grand style. According to the etiquette of the day, the arrangement terminated when the young man married one of his Creole contemporaries. However, his mistress —and of course, their children—would be financially set up for life. All of which is not to say that once a man was married he was forever true to his wife: Dalliances often came after the alliances, and wives usually looked the other way.

By the turn of the nineteenth century, the blending of cultures in the colony was well under way. At the time of the Louisiana Purchase, New Orleans had a population of about eight thousand—French and Spanish Creoles, Acadians, Germans, Americans, black slaves, and about thirteen hundred free people of color. (Incidentally, the aristocrats who had fled Santo Domingo looked down their noses at New Orleans Creoles, regarding them as "countrified.") The city also teemed with mysterious voodoo practitioners and swaggering pirates. Voodoo had been practiced in Louisiana since the first slaves were brought from West Africa, but after the arrival of the Haitian blacks voodoo rituals were common, albeit covert, events. As for the pirates, the most famous was Jean Lafitte, leader of a band of Baratarians (so called because their lair was in the waterways of Barataria Bay, south of the city).

Into this complex, mannered, rigidly stratified society barged the Americans. The first, who came downriver on keelboats and rafts, were generally roughnecks and roustabouts. Anything but dandies, these men, accustomed to working with their hands, came to the growing port to make plenty of money. Everything about them was appalling to the haughty Creoles: They were all riffraff. (Many of the newcomers were Scotch-Irish. The Gaelic word for rowing is *riffing*, and because they riffed their rafts down the river, they became known as riffraff.) To the Americans, the Creoles were stuck-up, lazy dandies. The Americans liked to hang around in coffeehouses, too; the difference is, they did their lolling *after* work while the Creoles lolled *in lieu* of work.

The Americanization of New Orleans ultimately led to statehood. In 1804 Congress divided the vast land of the Louisiana Purchase into the Territory of Louisiana and the Territory of Orleans. The boundaries of the Territory of Orleans matched those of the present-day state of Louisiana—minus West Florida, a large area of land between the Mississippi and Perdido Rivers. The history of West Florida is a story unto itself. In 1810, seventy American settlers north of Baton Rouge staged a revolt against Spanish rule and set up the Republic of West Florida. President James Madison immediately ordered Governor William C. C. Claiborne to move in and take possession. Claiborne established four parishes between the Mississippi and Pearl Rivers, thus inserting the instep in the Louisiana boot, and the boundaries of the state were set. In 1805 New Orleans was incorporated, and in 1812 Louisiana became the eighteenth state.

With statehood came the arrival of the first steamboat to successfully navigate the Mississippi, appropriately named the *New Orleans*. (A plaque near Washington

Artillery Park on Decatur Street marks the place where she docked.) Today the Mississippi is aslosh with riverboats for tourists, and by the end of 1994 there will be a veritable flotilla of riverboats for gamblers. (In 1991 the state legislature approved casino boats for the state's waterways.)

Fewer than three years after Louisiana became a state, the Battle of New Orleans—the last battle of the last war fought between England and the United States—was fought at Chalmette, five miles downriver of New Orleans. On January 8, 1815, none of the combatants were aware that two weeks earlier the adversaries had signed a peace treaty. The American forces, under the command of the wily Andrew Jackson, included Kentucky and Tennessee riflemen plus the Louisiana militia, free men of color, slaves, some of Lafitte's Baratarians, and Choctaw Indians. They were outnumbered five to three by crack British troops, fresh from the Peninsula Campaign, led by Sir Edward Pakenham. Fighting had broken out on December 14, 1814, and there were four engagements before the final battle. Moving across the green fields of Chalmette, near the banks of the Mississippi, the British attacked at sunrise. Wildly differing accounts abound of casualties on both sides, but all historians agree that American losses were minor and British casualties horrendous. On the American side, between six and thirteen men were killed and seventy-one injured; British casualties numbered about two thousand, and Pakenham himself was killed.

Beginning with the 1830s New Orleans became a boom town. The golden age lasted from the mid-nineteenth century up until the War Between the States. In 1820 about twenty-five thousand people lived in New Orleans; by 1840 more than one hundred thousand called the Crescent City home. Then the fourth-largest city in the nation, according to some accounts New Orleans was also the wealthiest. In 1835 the Carrollton Railway began operations, connecting downtown New Orleans not only with the City of Lafayette but with Carrollton farther upriver. Today the line still moves along the same route, but it's now the St. Charles Streetcar, a National Historic Landmark on tracks.

The enmity between the Americans and the Creoles continued to accelerate, however. A broad stretch of land between Iberville Street and the Commons (now marked by Common Street) had been set aside for a canal which was to connect the Mississippi with Lake Pontchartrain via the Carondelet Canal and Bayou St. John. The canal was never built, but the land that separated the feuding Creoles and Americans came to be known as the neutral ground, and the undug canal became Canal Street. (The wide median on Canal Street is still called the neutral ground by New Orleanians, as are all medians throughout the city. It's one of the city's several shibboleths.)

The continuing hostilities brought about the division of New Orleans into three separate municipalities: the First Municipality (the French Quarter), the Second Municipality (the American Sector), and the Third Municipality (an area downriver of the Quarter beginning at Esplanade Avenue). One mayor presided over the entire city, but each municipality had its own council. Not until 1852 were the municipalities consolidated—the Americans won out over their Creole rivals. The seat of government was moved from the Cabildo in the Place d'Armes to Gallier Hall on St. Charles Avenue in the American Sector.

Ten years later, New Orleans became an occupied city. Louisiana had seceded from the Union on March 21, 1861, and in the spring of the following year New Orleans suffered a Union naval attack commanded by Flag Officer David "Damn the Torpedoes" Farragut. On May 1, 1862, an occupying force under General Benjamin Butler marched into town, making New Orleans one of the first major Southern cities to fall. Although the state was readmitted to the Union in 1868, federal troops remained until 1877—longer than in any of the other Confederate states.

General Butler—known in New Orleans as "the Beast"—stayed in the city only until late 1862, but his is among the most hated of all names (townspeople also called him "Spoons" Butler; it was believed he had a penchant for pilfering silver). Although Butler has been credited with maintaining order and with scouring a city that had been filthy since its beginnings, locally he is best remembered for his "woman order." The ladies of New Orleans were rude to Yankee officers and would sometimes spit on them; Butler retaliated by announcing that any female who was disrespectful to the Yankee soldiers would be treated as a woman of the town plying her trade. (According to local legend, the ladies thereafter lined their chamber pots with pictures of the Beast.)

Since New Orleans fell so early in the war, it suffered relatively less than other Southern cities (Atlanta springs immediately to mind), although Reconstruction was marked by bloody riots and demonstrations. (Even so, in 1872, at the peak of that bitter period, the Rex organization staged its first Carnival parade.) Once Reconstruction was behind them, however, New Orleans' leaders put on the city's biggest bash ever: the World's Industrial and Cotton Centennial Exposition of 1884–85, held to commemorate the one-hundredth anniversary of the export of cotton. The exposition's buildings and attractions covered 250 acres of what is now Audubon Park, and pavilions were set up by countries from all over the globe. Despite high hopes and promises, however, the exposition was a financial as well as an artistic disaster.

Storyville, on the other hand—a well-meaning attempt by the city to contain prostitution—was a great success. Apparently the world's oldest profession had begun to flourish the minute the first female foot hit the muddy streets of Bienville's village; in 1744 a French officer remarked that there were not ten women of blameless character to be found in the entire city. In 1817 a $25 fine was levied on a certain girl who was "notoriously abandoned to lewdness." By 1857, in a form of taxation *personally* administered by the mayor, the city tried issuing licenses to madams ($250) and their girls ($100). "Sporting houses" flourished. In 1897 Alderman Sidney Story led the passage of an ordinance restricting the spread of bordellos to within about a twenty-block area behind the French Quarter. Much to the horror of the silk-stockinged Story, the district was christened Storyville and even had its own mayor—Tom Anderson, a state legislator. Blue Books—forerunners of the Yellow Pages —abounded; they offered listings and advertisements of the houses, the girls, and the girls' particular . . . talents. In great demand not only in New Orleans but in ports around the world, the Blue Books are still highly coveted —as collector's items. Storyville was shut down in 1917 on orders of the United States Navy; today a federal housing project stands on the site.

Not until the early twentieth century was a solution found for one of the city's other chronic problems: drainage. Because New Orleans lies below sea level and is surrounded by high levees, heavy rain and floodwaters can fill the bowl-shaped city. From its birth until early in this century, the city was plagued with yellow fever and malaria epidemics that claimed thousands of lives. As a result, seventy pumps in twenty strategically located stations throughout the city pull water from 180 miles of underground and open drainage canals into Lake Pontchartrain. (New Orleans has more canals than Venice.) With all the stops pulled out, so to speak, the pumps can create a flow of water equivalent to the nation's fifth-largest river.

Immigrants—thousands of Irish, Italians, and Germans—continued to pour into New Orleans throughout the nineteenth century. At the turn of the century the French Quarter was largely an Italian neighborhood. Today the city has upwards of two hundred thousand Sicilians; Yugoslavs, Greeks, Thais, and a sizeable Vietnamese community have added to the rich gumbo that is New Orleans.

PART TWO
••••••••••••
THE LIVING MUSEUM

Chapter Four

Jackson Square and the French Quarter

B IENVILLE would not be able to believe his eyes. When last *he* saw New Orleans, there wasn't so much as a paved street. Today there is nothing he would recognize—not even the oldest building, not even the river. In 1718, when Jean-Baptiste Le Moyne, Sieur de Bienville, founded the town he named la Nouvelle Or-léans, the Mississippi lapped at the levee that separated it from the Creoles promenading in the Place d'Armes. In those days, everything from Decatur Street to the river was *in* the river. Still, rivers have a way of changing course, and the Mississippi can be very cantankerous; gradually it began cozying up to the West Bank, leaving part of the East Bank high and dry. But then much has happened in the 275 years since Bienville carved a village out of canebrakes.

It's always easy to spot tourists in the French Quarter: They're the ones gazing around in wide-eyed wonder. (Locals are the ones with the smug looks.) Many first-time visitors to New Orleans expect great food and music, and in that they are not disappointed. They may

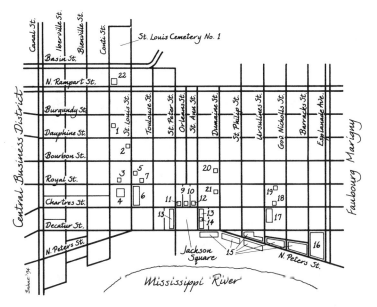

1. Musée Conti
2. Hermann-Grima House
3. Brennan's
4. Old Civil Courts
   Building
5. Antoine's
6. Omni Royal Orleans
7. Historic New Orleans
   Collection
8. St. Louis Cathedral
9. Pirate's Alley
10. Père Antoine's
    Alley
11. Cabildo
12. Presbytère
13. Pontalba Apts.
14. 1850 House
15. Old French Market
16. Old U.S. Mint
17. Old Ursuline
    Convent
18. Beauregard-Keyes
    House
19. Gallier House
20. Voodoo Museum
21. Madame John's
    Legacy
22. Our Lady of
    Guadalupe Church

The French Quarter

have heard of the topless/bottomless shows and the female impersonator revues on Bourbon. They may know that New Orleans, like Las Vegas, is a twenty-four-hour town with no legal closing time, and that folks walk around with plastic "go-cups" of booze. But the shock, oddly enough, is the architecture. Newcomers do not expect to be so utterly captivated by *houses* in a place known as a flat-out, rip-snorting party town.

But there they sit: row after row of quaint little town houses and cottages, dressed to kill in frilly gingerbread trim and lacy ironwork. Because of the nineteenth-century fires, most of them date from the early to mid-1800s. Almost all are one-, two-, or three-story structures; the sixteen-story Monteleone Hotel towers over them. Most are stucco houses painted in ice-cream colors or red-brick dwellings. Chimneys and dormer windows poke through high-pitched shingled roofs; gables jut up the sides of little cottages; wrought-iron balconies and galleries are virtually swathed in the greenery and flowers bursting out of hanging baskets. Most houses sit smack down on the banquette (called a sidewalk elsewhere) or have small stoops with two or three steps; doorways are adorned with graceful fanlights and colorful shutters. Scores of shops, funky jazz clubs, guesthouses, hole-in-the-wall bars and cafés, and ritzy restaurants are tucked into these erstwhile creole houses, their shutters flung open invitingly. The Quarter is awash with lush courtyards; Creoles would build a town house with a carriageway sweeping from the street alongside the front entrance to the rear courtyard. Many courtyards are hidden from the street, but, especially on Royal Street, poster or pastry shops are tucked away amid the banana trees and greenery.

The French Quarter is also known as the Vieux Carré, which means "old square." Its boundaries are Iberville Street, Rampart Street, Esplanade Avenue, and the Mississippi. In the early twentieth century the Quarter had fallen into a state of disrepair, and parts of it were slums. A preservationist named Elizabeth Werlein, horrified that the most important historic site in the city had been so neglected, began a drive to restore and save the site of Bienville's original village. Her efforts, along with those of others who joined her, were rewarded in 1936 when the Vieux Carré Commission was created by the state legislature and charged with preserving the original town.

Jackson Square, the French Quarter's centerpiece, forms the unmarked but acknowledged border between the upper and lower Quarter. Naturally, the river governs the directions. The upper Quarter—from St. Peter Street to Canal—is upriver of Jackson Square; the lower Quarter lies below—downriver of—the St. Ann Street border of the square. The upper Quarter is the section most frequented by tourists—most of Bourbon Street's bars are there—and the lower Quarter is a quieter, residential section.

The only way to properly explore the Quarter is on foot. But before beginning your stroll, soak up some of the history and color of the city in a fun and informative museum in the upper Quarter. The area code for all phone numbers is 504.

Musée Conti Wax Museum

This museum's series of historically accurate and remarkably lifelike tableaux make history come alive before your very eyes. The tale begins with La Salle's 1682 trip to the mouth of the Mississippi and continues on through the waxed clarinetist Pete Fountain—unofficial ambassador for the city, native son, and legend. The city's other legends are represented, too: Marie Laveau and her voodoo dancers, Andrew Jackson (depicted in the thick of the Battle of New Orleans), Jean Lafitte, Napoleon Bonaparte (seated in a bathtub), and a hundred others. The wax figures are garbed in handsome period costumes (except for Napoleon) and each tableau has a detailed caption.

At 917 Conti Street, the museum is open daily from

10:00 to 5:30. Admission is $5.70. Call 525-2605 for more information.

Hermann-Grima House

Samuel Hermann, a wealthy merchant, had this American-style brick town house built in 1831; in 1844 it was purchased by Judge Felix Grima. Judge Grima's family occupied the house for five generations; many family portraits adorn the walls. Guided tours take in the first floor, with its formal dining room, parlor, and bedrooms, and the rear outbuildings that line pretty parterre gardens. One of those rear buildings has a wonderful nineteenth-century kitchen with a huge open hearth, baking oven, and antique cooking utensils. Costumed docents do creole cooking demonstrations from October to May. And, yes, you get a little taste of creole fare.

Tickets can be purchased in the gift shop, which is housed in the former stable. At 820 St. Louis Street, it's open Monday through Saturday. Admission is $4. Call 525-5661 for more information. The sedate house museum is just a few steps from bawdy, gaudy Bourbon Street.

Bourbon Street

Bourbon—named for the French royal family and not, as you may surmise from its scent, for the alcoholic beverage—stretches from Canal Street to Esplanade Avenue, exposing itself for all the world to see. It is remarkably tame during the day; if you hadn't been on the street the night before you might wonder why all those people are out hosing down their sidewalks in the morning. New Orleans has always been naughty, and the revelers who reel along Bourbon in the wee hours wouldn't damage her reputation for anything. (Incidentally, it is illegal to carry open glass or metal containers on the streets; that's why the city is aslosh with plastic go-cups.) During special events (New Year's Eve, the Sugar Bowl, Mardi Gras) Bourbon is *the* place to be—depending upon your tolerance for nonstop screaming. But Bourbon has many faces. Galatoire's, one of the city's finest French creole restaurants, and the Royal Sonesta Hotel, in the next block, both maintain a serene, sophisticated presence. Prominent people live in Bourbon's quieter residential district, in the lower Quarter. Stop at the corner of Bourbon and Toulouse and read the plaque on the wall of the Inn on Bourbon: The French Opera House, one of the grandest in the land, stood on this site from 1859 until it burned slap to the ground in 1919.

Royal Street

A block from Bourbon, Royal Street—light years away in ambience—is famed for its many art galleries and expensive antique stores. In the nineteenth century Royal's 300 and 400 blocks were a banking center (several of the prestigious antique shops are housed in former bank buildings). The large pink Greek Revival building at 334 Royal, now home to the French Quarter police station, was built in 1826 for the Bank of Louisiana, and Brennan's Restaurant, at 417 Royal, was home in 1805 to the Banque de la Louisiane. Across the street, the large granite and marble building was built just after the turn of the century as the Civil Courts Building. Among the buildings razed to make way for this mammoth baroque structure was the original home of Antoine's Restaurant (now at 713 St. Louis Street, a half block away).

Old St. Louis Exchange Hotel (Omni Royal Orleans)

If you go into the white marbled halls of the Royal O, on 621 St. Louis Street, you can see a large painting of the famous St. Louis Exchange Hotel that stood on this site in the 1830s. The hotel was the work of J. N. B. de Pouilly, one of several prominent architects working in the city in the 1830s during the city's golden age; he designed the houses in Exchange Alley, the Olivier House Hotel, and several of the elaborate tombs in the St. Louis Cemeteries. The St. Louis Hotel, which was grand indeed, was the social center for the Creoles. The hotel was razed in 1916; the Royal Orleans was built in 1960.

Historic New Orleans Collection

One of the nation's largest private collections of historic materials is housed in a complex that includes the 1792 Merieult House, a Spanish colonial home that survived the fire of 1794. Over a period of many years, the late Kemper and Leila Williams amassed a vast collection of historic documents, manuscripts, maps, letters, and about two hundred thousand paintings, photographs, prints, and drawings. The Williams Gallery (free to the public) displays changing exhibits drawn from the collection. Guided tours of the complex (fee is $2) include the Merieult House (which has a colorful past), the research facilities and library, and the Williams' handsomely furnished cottage.

The complex, which is on 533 Royal, is open Tuesday through Saturday from 10:00 to 4:45. For more information call 523-4662. A stroll down St. Louis Street toward the river will bring you to Chartres Street. At the corner of Chartres and St. Louis is the Napoleon House, a fine place to stop for a Pimm's Cup or a cappuccino (see Chapter 14).

Old Pharmacy Museum

The colorful apothecary jars in the windows offer just a glimpse of what's inside this musty little museum. In

HISTORICAL HIGHLIGHTS

History buffs might like to try this French Quarter tour.

◆ *Old Ursuline Convent (1114 Chartres)*— the oldest building in the lower Mississippi valley.

◆ *Madame John's Legacy (632 Dumaine)*— an eighteenth-century house that *might* pre-date the convent.

◆ *Jackson Square*—Visit the Cabildo and Presbytère (eighteenth-century) and St. Louis Cathedral, 1850 House, and Pontalba Apartments (nineteenth-century structures).

◆ *Historic New Orleans Collection (533 Royal)*—Tour historic Merieult House to see collection of paintings, documents, maps, and much more.

◆ *Musée Conti Wax Museum (917 Conti)*— colorful tableaux of Louisiana legends.

◆ *Napoleon House (500 Chartres)*—Munch a lunch of warm muffulettas in this historic building.

See Chapter 11 for more history stops.

1823 Louis J. Dufilho, Jr. lived upstairs and ran his apothecary shop downstairs. (Dufilho, who was licensed in 1816, is said to have been the nation's first licensed pharmacist.) The shop is crammed full of nineteenth-century dental equipment, medical implements, prescriptions, and everything from leech jars to voodoo charms to cosmetics. A big attraction is the Italian marble soda fountain, which dates from 1855. In the rear courtyard you can see where Dufilho grew herbs and things of a medicinal nature.

The museum, at 514 Chartres Street, is open daily (except Monday) from 10:00 to 5:00 (565-8027). Admission is $3. The tool around the upper Quarter ends at Jackson Square, the heart of the Vieux Carré.

Jackson Square

In 1721, when Adrien de Pauger laid out the square, it was called the Place d'Armes and was used as a parade grounds for the militia. At that time it was a large, perfectly square, totally treeless village green that opened onto the river. Barracks for the militia lined each side, where now stand the Pontalba Apartments.

The history of New Orleans has been virtually played out in this old square. In the early days, public executions and exquisite punishments took place here. In 1803, ceremonies in the square accompanied the signing of papers for the Louisiana Purchase, which took place in the Sala Capitular of the Cabildo. Andrew Jackson was given a hero's welcome here after his victory in the Battle of New Orleans. (Each January 8, ceremonies in the square and the cathedral commemorate the famous battle.) In 1825, when Lafayette visited New Orleans, and in 1847, when Zachary Taylor came to town, triumphal arches of monumental proportions were erected in the square.

The Place d'Armes was officially changed to Jackson Square on January 28, 1851. In 1840, President Andrew Jackson himself laid the cornerstone for a monument that would finally be dedicated on February 9, 1856: the colossal bronze statue of the general on a rearing horse, by the sculptor Clark Mills. This is one of three such statues of Jackson; the others are in Washington and Nashville. (The inscription on the statue's base—"The Union Must and Shall Be Preserved"—was engraved during the Union occupation by order of the Yankee general "Beast" Butler.) The present-day square, surrounded by an ornate cast-iron fence, began to take shape in 1851. The mall surrounding the square was paved with flagstones in 1975, and the square itself is beautifully landscaped with flower beds and trees. Tucked in each corner, scarcely visible because of the greenery, are small white marble statues that represent the four seasons.

The mall is a busy place, where sidewalk portraitists and caricaturists work and display their wares on the iron fence and mimes and clowns entertain tourists. (Most of the street musicians have been banished to Woldenberg Riverfront Park, a result of complaints by residents in the Pontalba Apartments.) A good place to get an overview of the square is from Washington Artillery Park, across Decatur Street. You can get close to Old Man River by strolling across the streetcar tracks (keeping an eye out for streetcars) to Moonwalk; the wooden promenade is a great place to watch the tugs, freighters, ferries, and riverboats. (Panhandlers and pickpockets are also lured to the boardwalk, so be alert.)

St. Louis Cathedral

In 1993 the archdiocese of New Orleans celebrated its two hundredth anniversary. The first church of the Parish of St. Louis—named for Louis IX, France's saint-king—was designed by Adrien de Pauger, the engineer who laid out the streets of the village in 1721. (De Pauger died in 1726, before the church was finished; according to his wishes, he was buried beneath the church floor.) A second church was destroyed in the fire of Good Friday in 1788.

The present-day church, the third to stand on this site, had its first services on Christmas Eve, 1794, when it was dedicated as a cathedral. In 1851 the church was enlarged considerably by architect J. N. B. de Pouilly. (During the reconstruction the central tower collapsed, precipitating in short order the dismissal of de Pouilly, much finger pointing, and lawsuits.)

Napoleon's many New Orleans admirers staged a "funeral" for him here, replete with an elaborately decorated catafalque. Four years later, in 1829, funeral services were held for the beloved Père Antoine (the Spaniard Antonio de Sedella), the Capuchin priest who had served the church for more than forty years. In 1872 Alsatian artist Erasme Humbrecht painted the large mural behind the main altar of St. Louis announcing the Seventh Crusade; the mural was completely refurbished in 1938. Pope Paul VI designated the cathedral a Minor Basilica in 1964, and when Pope John Paul II visited New Orleans in 1987, the flagstone plaza in front of the church was christened Place Jean Paul Deux. Tours are conducted daily except during services.

Just behind the church lies St. Anthony's Garden, also known as Cathedral Gardens. Sycamore, oak, and magnolia trees shade a statue of the Sacred Heart of Jesus and a small white obelisk that pays tribute to thirty French sailors who died near New Orleans following an outbreak of yellow fever in Mexico. Peaceful as it is now, this little park was a favored spot for Creole duels in Colonial days. The twin flagstone alleys—Pirate's Alley and Père Antoine's Alley—that laze alongside the cathedral and the garden were cut in the 1830s. The Faulkner House Bookstore, at 624 Pirate's Alley, occupies the house wherein William Faulkner wrote his first novel, *Soldiers' Pay*, in 1925.

Cabildo and Presbytère

The two almost identical buildings that flank St. Louis Cathedral are the Cabildo (on your left as you face the church) and the Presbytère. Both buildings, which date from the 1790s, replaced earlier structures that were destroyed in the 1788 fire. The Cabildo, one of the most important of the state's historical buildings, housed the Spanish town council (*cabildo*); it was here that transfer papers for the Louisiana Purchase were signed on December 20, 1803. This building served as city hall for the Creoles when New Orleans was divided into three separate municipalities in the nineteenth century. Ironically, almost two hundred years to the month after the 1788 fire, the Cabildo was again ablaze. Mercifully, the 1988 fire only damaged the roof (the treasures within were salvaged). Restoration was a long process, but the Cabildo reopened to great acclaim in February 1994. The Cabildo, one of the state's most important museums, contains an extensive collection of historic documents pertaining to the region as well as a death mask of Napoleon, paintings, maps, and memorabilia.

The Presbytère, on the downriver side of the cathedral, never served its original purpose—as the rectory of the church. The city purchased the building in 1835, and for a time it was used as a courthouse. Now, like the Cabildo, it houses changing exhibits.

Both buildings are on Chartres Street at Jackson Square. The Cabildo, the Presbytère, and the 1850 House (all on Jackson Square), as well as the old U. S. Mint on Esplanade Avenue, are part of the Louisiana State Museum complex. All are open Tuesday through Sunday from 10:00 to 5:00. Admission to each is $4, and a combination ticket for all four museums can be purchased for $12. For additional information call 568-6972.

Pontalba Apartments

Said to be among the oldest apartment buildings in the country, the Pontalbas were built between 1849 and 1851 thanks to the efforts of the Baroness de Pontalba, the daughter of the city's benefactor, Don Andres Almonester y Roxas. The twin three-story brick buildings that face each other across Jackson Square are graced with some of the loveliest ironwork in the city. (The initials AP, for Almonester/Pontalba, are woven into the grillwork.) Now, as they were when originally built, the Pontalbas have shops and restaurants on the ground level and apartments on the second and third levels. Not surprisingly, this being New Orleans, a good many of the Pontalba shops involve food; Angelo Brocato's, in the lower Pontalbas, is a good place to stop in for a refreshing Italian ice. A few steps away is the New Orleans Welcome Center (529 St. Ann), which has a plethora of free maps and brochures.

1850 House

The Pontalba apartments are private residences and are not open to the public. However, a three-story apartment in the lower Pontalbas has been restored and dressed up to illustrate the lifestyle of an uppercrust Creole family of 1850. This wonderful peek into the past displays hand-some carved armoires, canopy beds, formal dining room, and antique kitchen. (Some of the furnishings were the work of Mallard and Seignoret, two esteemed cabinet-makers in nineteenth-century New Orleans.) On the ground floor, the Friends of the Cabildo bookstore has a wealth of books about the city.

The 1850 House, a property of the Louisiana State Museum, has the same operating hours and admissions as the Cabildo, the Presbytère, and the Old U. S. Mint. Turn left after leaving the 1850 House to begin a stroll through the lower Quarter, beginning with the Old French Market.

Old French Market

Café du Monde, on St. Ann and Decatur, is the upriver anchor of the French Market and the city's favorite spot for people-watching. Reminiscent of the great European sidewalk cafés, it is open twenty-four hours and turns out zillions of beignets and oceans of *café au lait*. It has been on this stand for well over a hundred years. This building, a meat market in 1813, is the oldest in the French Market complex. It replaced a Spanish structure that was built after the 1788 fire and was itself swept away by a hurricane. The eighteenth-century version of a mall without a multiplex, it was the place where the colonists came to get both food and gossip. But even before there was a building, an Indian trading post sat on this site in the 1600s.

The French Market today is abuzz with activity; shops of all sorts are tucked in its arcades and colonnades, and there are several open-air cafés for taking life easy and listening to jazz. In Dutch Alley, at the foot of Dumaine Street, free concerts are regularly scheduled. Here the street divides, with Decatur driving dead ahead and North Peters Street veering off into French Market Place. At 914–16 North Peters, the Folklife Center of the Jean Lafitte National Historical Park Service has displays pertaining to New Orleans and regional culture; this is the jumping-off place for the tours conducted by the park rangers. A block farther downriver, the Farmer's Market, its open sheds filled with fresh country produce, stretches as far as the Old U. S. Mint. A sixties-style flea market, open from dawn to dusk, is between Governor Nicholls and Barracks Streets. Jimmy Buffett's Margaritaville is in this area, as is the Palm Court Jazz Café. After the

Louisiana Purchase, Gallatin Street occupied what is now French Market Place. Said to have been known to sailors all over the world, it was one of the wildest, meanest, most low-down evil areas in the world. Not a trace of the street remains.

Old U. S. Mint

When you reach the end of Farmer's Market, you'll be at the rear entrance of the Old U. S. Mint, which sits at the downriver border of the Quarter. The massive building, with its Greek Revival portico, was built in 1835 to house a branch of the federal mint. In its day—which lasted until 1861, when the War Between the States broke out —the mint churned out nearly $300 million in coins. During Reconstruction it was used as an assay office, and in 1879 it once again began to mint—an activity that ended for good in 1909. Now a property of the Louisiana State Museum complex, it houses two exhibits of vital importance to New Orleans: the Jazz Exhibit, which traces the history of the city's most famous music idiom and the Mardi Gras Exhibit, which displays glittery Carnival memorabilia. Another exhibit traces the history of the building itself.

The mint is at 400 Esplanade Avenue and is open Tuesday through Sunday from 10:00 to 5:00. Admission is $4. Call 568-6972 or 568-6968 for more information. At Esplanade Avenue the Riverfront Streetcar begins its rumble upriver, making stops at Jackson Square, the aquarium, Riverwalk, and other notable destinations.

Faubourg Marigny

Faubourg Marigny—named for Bernard de Marigny, who had a vast plantation here and was one of the city's most colorful characters—begins at Esplanade Avenue and lolls downriver. In 1800, when Bernard was fifteen years old, his father died and left him a fortune. Alas, the lad led a profligate life, frittering away his inheritance in this country and in Europe. In 1805 Marigny subdivided his plantation into lots and the section became another *faubourg*—the second-oldest suburb after Faubourg Ste. Marie, across Canal Street. Faubourg Marigny was the Third Municipality in 1835, when the city was officially divided. Today it's a predominantly residential area with a jumble of streets totally divergent from the Quarter's grid. It is home to several excellent restaurants—the Praline Connection among them—and to popular night-spots such as The Mint, Snug Harbor, and Café Brasil (see Chapter 16). Esplanade Avenue, a boulevard shaded with magnificent trees, was once one of the grandest streets in the city. In 1876 the French impressionist Edgar Degas stayed and painted at 2306 Esplanade, the home of his New Orleanian mother. Sadly, many of the Esplanade's fine old mansions have deteriorated.

Doubling back into the Quarter from Esplanade, walk three blocks along Chartres to see the city's oldest site, the Old Ursuline Convent.

Old Ursuline Convent

This big, marvelously creaky old building is all that remains of Bienville's original village. The most important structure not only in New Orleans but in the lower Mississippi valley, the convent was begun in 1745, completed in 1752, and has survived the conflagrations of 1788 and 1794. (In 1788 Père Antoine, then rector of St. Louis Cathedral, rushed to the convent and organized a bucket brigade to save the building.) Recent research has revealed that it is the second Ursuline convent to occupy this site, the first having been completed in 1734. (The first building was the one occupied by the Ursuline nuns who arrived from Rouen in 1727; they stayed elsewhere until it was built.) The handhewn spiral cypress stairs just inside the main building are from that original building, and an iron cross in the landscaped courtyard came with the sisters from Rouen.

Included in a tour of the compound is the Our Lady of Victory Church, in which gilt fleurs-de-lis decorate the pine-and-cypress ceiling. Overlooking the impressive altar is a statue of Mother Cabrini, who once walked the halls of the convent. Other life-size statues, of St. Peter and St. Paul, were removed from St. Louis Cathedral and placed here. Windows are handpainted rather than stained; one depicts Our Lady of Prompt Succor, beneath which is a small scene of the Battle of New Orleans. During that battle the sisters prayed fervently for a swift victory, and Andrew Jackson personally called on the nuns to thank them for their help. In the convent the Ursulines conducted an orphanage, school, and hospital. The complex is dedicated to Archbishop Antoine Blanc, the first archbishop of the diocese.

The complex is located at 1100 Chartres Street. Tours (fee is $4) are conducted on the hour (except for noon) Tuesday through Friday from 10:00 to 3:00, and Saturday and Sunday at 11:15, 1:00 and 2:00. For further information call 529-3040.

Beauregard-Keyes House

Directly across the street from the convent, this house museum, with its handsome Greek Revival portico, dates from 1826. After the War Between the States, Confederate general P. G. T. Beauregard—"the Great Creole"— occupied the house for a short while. The Keyes part of the name is novelist Frances Parkinson Keyes, who purchased the house in 1944 to save it from demolition; she lived and wrote in the restored rear servants' quarters.

CULTURE

The Quarter has something to offer to those with a cultural bent.

♦ *Royal Street* for antique shops and art galleries.
♦ *House museums*: Hermann-Grima House (820 St. Louis), Gallier House (1118–32 Royal), and Beauregard-Keyes House (1113 Chartres).

See Chapters 5, 8, and 11 for other cultural treats.

(Keyes' mystery novel *Dinner at Antoine's* is a great, albeit dated, book to read before visiting the city.) Today docents guide visitors through the house and servants' quarters, and a visit to the lovely English garden adjacent to the house is included in the admission.

The house is at 1113 Chartres Street. Tours are conducted daily (except Sunday) on the hour from 10:00 to 3:00. Admission is $4. Phone 523-7257 for more information. One block away from the river, on Royal Street, is another of the Quarter's house museums.

Gallier House

Each of the house museums has its own distinct personality; if you've seen one you've definitely not seen them all. The Gallier House was designed and built in 1857 by architect James Gallier, Jr., as his family home. The front galleries are dolled up with lovely, lacy ironwork and the interior is splendidly decorated with period furnishings.

Gallier senior and his son were among the city's most highly regarded architects in the nineteenth century. Gallier senior, born James Gallagher in Ireland, came to New Orleans via New York; he changed his name to Gallier to blend in with the French Creoles. Special film exhibits in the house include demonstrations on the art of creating decorative *faux marbre* and *faux bois* (false marble and false wood).

The house is at 1118–32 Royal Street. Tours are conducted daily (except Sunday) from 10:30 to 3:45. Admission is $4. For more information phone 523-6722.

Lafitte's Blacksmith Shop

You'll not get your horse shod here, nor will you be able to shop for anything other than beverages. A neighborhood bar for ages, this house, like many another in New Orleans, has its legend. The persistent story has it that freebooter Jean Lafitte and his brother, Pierre, operated a blacksmith shop here as a front for their smuggling and other nefarious deeds. Of course, not a trace of evidence supports that belief—but then there are not a whale of a lot of people around that can prove anything one way or the other. Ownership records of the house go back to 1772, but it is not known when it was built. Interestingly, the tumbledown cottage is one of the very few extant examples of brick-between-posts construction, the building method employed by the French Creoles. Because it bears no resemblance to the houses built by the Spanish after the great fires, the possibility exists that this house could, like the Old Ursuline Convent, be a survivor of Bienville's village. In any case, the dark, grungy little house, located at 941 Bourbon Street, is a great place for soaking up Old World atmosphere—and, of course, for knocking back a few adult beverages.

Voodoo Museum

Very few people in New Orleans actually know whether voodoo is still seriously practiced; among those who insist that it is are the operators of this dark and mysterious museum. The little front room is lined with glass cases filled with voodoo accoutrements, including *gris-gris* (pronounced gree-gree, meaning "charms"). The back room is graced with a voodoo altar and done up with a variety of artifacts pertaining to the cult—or religion, as practitioners prefer to call it. Voodoo arrived with slaves from West Africa, and the practice grew when refugees from Santo Domingo came to New Orleans at the turn of the nineteenth century. Marie Laveau is the best-known voodoo queen, and a large portrait of her is prominently displayed here.

The museum, which is located at 724 Dumaine Street, offers a variety of voodoo tours. It is open daily from 10:00 to 7:00. Admission is $5. Phone 523-7685 for more information.

Madame John's Legacy

Unfortunately, this wonderful West Indies-style house, on 632 Dumaine, can only be admired from the street; it is a property of the Louisiana State Museum but is not open to the public. Some historians insist that this building is a survivor from Bienville's village and is even older than the Old Ursuline Convent, based on their belief that parts of a house that stood here in 1724 survived the fire of 1788 and that those parts were incorporated in this house. (Other historians contend that the house was completely destroyed and rebuilt in 1788 immediately after the fire.) Madame John was a fictional character in a short story, " 'Tite Poulette," by nineteenth-century New Orleans writer George Washington Cable. Cable wrote caustic tales about the Creoles; among the other houses that figure in his stories are the First Skyscraper at 640 Royal Street, which is also called 'Sieur George after a character in a story by the same name.

North Rampart and Basin Streets

For many years North Rampart Street, which forms the back border of the French Quarter, has been an eyesore,

---

VOODOO TO DO

Voodoo dabblers shouldn't miss these Quarter sights.

- *New Orleans Voodoo Museum (724 Dumaine)*—an overview and history of Crescent City voodoo.
- *Hello, Dolly (815 Royal)*—a large collection of voodoo dolls, some designed by extraterrestrial beings.
- *Mystic Curio (833 Royal)*—voodoo oils, potions, occult books, readings, unusual jewelry.
- *Poo Ella's (627 Dumaine)*—voodoo/tarot cards and readings.
- *Blue Bayou (521 St. Philip)*—a witchcraft shop, with voodoo oils, potions, powders, ju-ju bags, and many other voodoo accoutrements.
- *Magic Cemetery Walk (593-9693)*—Group tours take in the above-ground tomb of Marie Laveau, legendary nineteenth-century voodoo queen.

and a dangerous one at that. Louis Armstrong Park, whose glittering entrance is at St. Ann Street, has long been a hangout for muggers and drug users. But the park is also the site of the Cultural Center—Municipal Auditorium and the Theatre for the Performing Arts; the former has been the scene of countless Carnival balls, the latter the home of the New Orleans Opera and the New Orleans City Ballet. In late 1993 changes seemed to be afoot for the park. Municipal Auditorium may be home to a temporary casino ("temporary" possibly meaning two years plus). A huge casino is to be built at the foot of Canal; in 1993 it was estimated that the building would be completed sometime in 1995. Virtually everything regarding the casino is iffy—except for its being enormously controversial.

Because of its location, Our Lady of Guadalupe Church (411 N. Rampart) is best visited with a tour. The church was built in 1826 as the Mortuary Chapel, where funeral services were held for yellow fever victims; New Orleans had many outbreaks of "bronze John" or "yellow Jack," as the disease was called. Among the saints in this church is one St. Expedite: An old, old legend has it that one day a crate arrived at the church marked simply "Expedite!"; the figure was then expeditiously unpacked and mounted on the wall. The other, less frequently told, tale is that St. Expedite figures prominently in voodoo lore. This church, also known as the voodoo church, is one of the stops on tours conducted by the Voodoo Museum.

Behind the church, on Basin Street, is St. Louis Cemetery No. 1, the city's oldest extant cemetery, dating from 1789, shortly after the great fire (the earliest cemetery was on the site of present-day St. Peter Street). Many visitors are intrigued by New Orleans' unique Cities of the Dead, as these graveyards are called; the whitewashed tombs and mausoleums look for all the world like miniature houses, and well-worn brick pathways lead through them. Prior to modern-day drainage systems, burials in New Orleans had to be above ground; with most of the city lying below sea level, below-ground burials often resulted in caskets bobbing merrily back to the surface. Many of the city's earliest notables are buried in St. Louis Cemetery No. 1.

Four blocks beyond this cemetery is St. Louis Cemetery No. 2, many of whose elaborate tombs were designed by J. N. B. de Pouilly; de Pouilly arrived in New Orleans in the 1830s with a sketchbook filled with drawings of the famed Père Lachaise Cemetery in Paris. Many of the tombs and temples are as dressed up as the frilly houses in the French Quarter. St. Louis Cemetery No. 3, on Esplanade Avenue near City Park, is the largest of the three St. Louis cemeteries. Although the cemeteries are a major attraction, they are also very unsafe. *Do not visit any of these cemeteries alone*; there have been numerous muggings and other unpleasant, often drug-related incidents. The organization Save Our Cemeteries (588-9357) does ninety-minute guided tours of cemetery no. 1.

Adjacent to cemetery no. 1 is the Iberville Housing Project—a good place to avoid. The project occupies the site of Storyville, the tenderloin district that flourished from 1897 until 1917. But please do not go in search of remnants of the red-light district; absolutely nothing— not a trace—remains.

Chapter Five

♦♦♦♦♦♦♦♦♦♦♦

Stepping on the Foot
of Canal

T HE CITY'S Central Business District—the CBD—
is adjacent to the French Quarter, with Canal
Street dividing uptown from downtown. The CBD's skyscrapers, convention hotels, monuments, and stores
sprouted up out of former sugar plantations. Try to
picture a time 275 years ago when Canal was a dirt strip
of land 171 feet wide, with a green commons beginning
at Common Street.

In the early eighteenth century Bienville's plantation
extended upriver from the commons. After the 1788 fire,
Bertrand Gravier, who had obtained the land once occupied by Bienville's plantation and later by a Jesuit plantation, began to subdivide his property into lots. Gravier
called this new suburb, the city's first, Faubourg Ste.
Marie, after his wife. The Vieux Carré, or French Quarter, was virtually a blackened wasteland after the fire, so
some Creoles began to move there. But as more and more
Americans came in after the signing of the 1803 Louisiana Purchase, the subdivision became known as Faubourg
St. Mary.

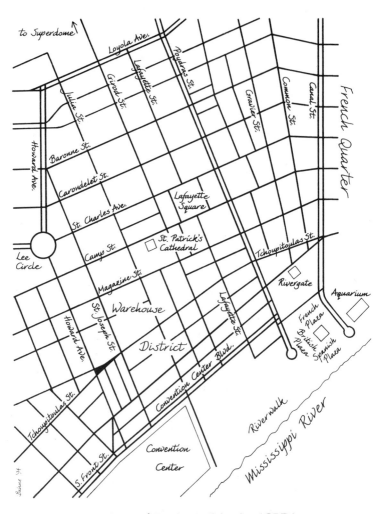

Central Business District (CBD)

Although Frenchman J. N. B. de Pouilly was the architect of choice for the Creoles in the French Quarter, Irish and Yankee architects designed the structures in the burgeoning American Sector; by the 1830s—the beginning of the city's golden age—the American Sector had sprawled farther upriver. The Carrollton Railway began rolling in 1835; known today as the St. Charles Streetcar, it's the oldest street railway system in the world, a National Historic Landmark, and an excellent way to get to the Garden District and uptown.

A good place to get an overview of the city is from Viewpoint, the observation tower on the thirty-first floor of the World Trade Center (2 Canal Street), which affords a 360-degree panorama of the city and the Mississippi. As you face the river, "downriver" is to your left, and you can clearly see the river's great bend at Algiers Point. To your right, just "upriver," is the Crescent City Connection, the bridge that connects the East and West Banks. (Algiers, an old residential district of the city, is on the West Bank, which is due east of the East Bank.) Between you and the bridge sprawls brightly colored Spanish Plaza, where several riverboats tie up, and just beyond it are Riverwalk and the Ernest N. Morial Convention Center. Almost beneath your feet is the Canal Street Ferry, which makes the run back and forth—"across-river," if you will—between the foot of Canal and Algiers. Looking out over the city, with downriver now to your right, you can see the sloping rooftops of the French Quarter and the spires of St. Louis Cathedral.

Still from Viewpoint, smack below your toes is the foot of Canal, for which (at this writing, anyway) great changes are planned. The Rivergate Exhibition Center, directly across the street from the World Trade Center, is destined to be transformed into the "world's largest casino." (At press time discussions were still underway between the city and Harrah's Jazz, which will operate the casino, as to whether the Rivergate will be demolished or simply remodeled to accommodate the casino.) In the far distance, Lake Pontchartrain is the broad blue swath across the horizon and City Park is the big patch of green on its south shore. Mid-City is the huge section that snoozes between the French Quarter and the lake. The CBD extends from Canal upriver to Howard Avenue, and from the river roughly to Loyola Avenue on the lakeside. Within the boundaries of the CBD, between Girod and Howard Avenue, lies the Warehouse District, an area of abandoned warehouses that are being renovated as art galleries and restaurants. Just beyond Loyola hunkers the Louisiana Superdome, home of the New Orleans Saints. Poydras Street, which would parallel Canal if the CBD were laid out as sensibly as the French Quarter, barrels from the foot of the CBD and roars past the Dome. The Garden District and uptown roll along upriver of Howard Avenue, beyond the Warehouse District. Farther beyond uptown are the plantations along the Great River Road, and about 130 miles farther lies Lafayette, in the heart of Cajun Country.

You can purchase Viewpoint tickets for $2 in the lobby of the World Trade Center; catch the glass elevator to reach the observation tower. The tower is open daily from 9:00 to 5:00. For more information call 525-2185. The area code for all phone numbers in this chapter is 504.

Aquarium of the Americas

Even folks who are not necessarily fish people are impressed by the aquarium, which made a huge splash when it opened on Labor Day of 1990. There is a slew of touch tanks, demonstrations, feedings, and hands-on exhibits, as well as a café, but the four main exhibits are the 132,000-gallon Caribbean Reef, with a transparent tunnel through which you can stroll and look up at the sea critters; the mist-filled Amazon Rain Forest, with its high humidity, tropical birds, anaconda, piranha, replica Cajun trapper's cabin, and twenty-foot waterfall; the Mississippi River/Gulf Shores, with its white alligators, hundred-pound flathead catfish, and displays of Louisiana's rapidly vanishing wetlands; and the Gulf of Mexico, in which a fabricated oil rig shows how various species of sea creatures flourish in such artificial reefs and sixteen-foot acrylic panels let you go eyeball-to-eyeball with tarpon, tiger sharks, and amberjack. Just outside the Amazon exhibit is the Living in Water area (its penguins are a popular attraction). In addition to its permanent exhibits the aquarium hosts traveling shows such as the 1993 shark exhibit.

The aquarium is located at Canal Street and the river. It opens daily at 9:30, and closes at 6:00 Sunday through Thursday and at 7:00 Friday and Saturday (at various times during the summer it stays open until 9:00). Admission is $9.25. Call 861-2537 for more information.

Woldenberg Riverfront Park

Surrounding the aquarium and extending to the Jackson Brewery at Jackson Square, this sixteen-acre park offers a broad open space with trees, park benches (with seated statuary), and brick walkways that follow alongside the river. Street musicians, clowns, mimes, and shoeshine vendors are often hard at work. The park is patrolled night and day and is lit at night. The aquarium and the park, incidentally, sit right on the crescent that gave the Crescent City its nickname.

The development of the aquarium and the riverfront park are part of a long-term project known as Riverfront 2000. The Audubon Institute, which operates the aquarium and the Audubon Zoo, plans six other facilities that will open in several phases up to the end of the millennium. Included is a $20 million expansion of the aquarium, a $40 million Natural History Museum, a $17 million model zoo for environmental education, and a Species Survival Center.

Mardi Gras World

The landing for the Canal Street Ferry is just across Canal from the aquarium. The ferry sallies fro and to Algiers,

---

NATURAL NEW ORLEANS

Those who enjoy seeing or learning about the great outdoors will want to catch these attractions.

◆ *Aquarium of the Americas*
◆ *Woldenberg Riverfront Park*
◆ *Lafayette Square*

See Chapters 6, 7, 8, 10, and 11 for other natural highs.

---

serving as a commuter vessel for those who live in that area and work downtown. It's a delightful, breezy outing as well, and the whole venture takes less than a half hour. (The round trip is free for pedestrians; the return fare for vehicles is a dollar.) Blaine Kern's Mardi Gras World in Algiers is home to the world's largest float builder. In huge warehouses known as dens, Kern and crew create gigantic, fanciful Mardi Gras floats. A great place to bring kids, this is a fantasyland where artisans fashion the floats' massive papier-mâché figures and colorful scenes that are part and parcel of Carnival. (Kern also designs and builds floats for Macy's Thanksgiving day parade.)

Free shuttles from Mardi Gras World (223 Newton Street) meet each ferry and take you right to its door. It's open every day (except Mardi Gras) from 9:30 to 4:30. Admission is $4.50. The phone number is 362-8211.

International Plazas

Back on the East Bank, the foot of Canal is decorated with four plazas that were gifts to the city from countries that have played a major part in its history. Spanish Plaza, adjacent to the ferry landing, is a broad, mosaic-tiled plaza that was a bicentennial gift to the city. Waters gush fifty feet high from a huge circular fountain that has walls imbedded with colorful Spanish coats of arms. Kiosks sell tickets for the riverboats that tie up at the Poydras Street Wharf, and the Riverwalk shopping mall rolls out just upriver. The largest and splashiest of the four plazas, Spain's gift is the scene of a grand and glorious masked ball on Lundi Gras (Fat Monday, or Mardi Gras eve). The only "ticket" required for the free bash is a mask, and fireworks, music, and the year's first appearance of Rex, King of Carnival, are among its attractions.

Across from the World Trade Center, Place de France features a small but glittery statue of Joan of Arc that was presented by Charles de Gaulle during a 1960 visit. A block away, England's contribution sits near the Hilton on a patch of green called British Place: a nine-foot bronze statue of a cigar-wielding Winston Churchill. The tribute to the city's many Italians, Piazza d'Italia, at the corner of Tchoupitoulas and Poydras, is the scene of a street festival each Columbus Day.

U. S. Customhouse

The huge, grey, Egyptianesque structure hunkering over the entire 400 block of Canal hordes one of the city's great treasures. The Great Marble Hall, which the American Institute of Architects calls one of the nation's most important examples of Greek Revival architecture, will take your breath away—if you've any left after the steep two-story climb. A skylight of wood, iron, and glass hovers 54 feet above a floor that measures 95 feet by 125 feet. Supporting the skylight are fourteen white Italian marble Corinthian columns, each one 41 feet high with a girth of 4 feet. The great marble bas-relief on the river side of the hall depicts Jean Baptiste Le Moyne, Sieur de Bienville, the city's founder, and Andrew Jackson, its savior and hero, flanking the Great Seal of Louisiana. Over the Canal Street entrance an American Eagle and the shield of the U. S. government are captured in one of two lovely stained-glass windows; in the other, the pelican, Louisiana's state bird, is shown with the state's seal. The mammoth building was begun in 1845, was interrupted by the Civil War, and was not completed until 1881. During the war the partially constructed building served as headquarters for Union forces under General Benjamin "Beast" Butler; it also housed two thousand Confederate prisoners.

The hall is located at 423 Canal. It is open free of charge Monday through Friday from 9:00 to 5:00.

ARCHITECTURAL GEMS

Architecture lovers should map out these sights for any Canal Street touring.

• *Old U. S. Customhouse (423 Canal)*— Great Marble Hall, a monumental Greek Revival masterpiece on the third floor.
• *Gallier Hall (545 St. Charles)*—another splendid example of Greek Revival architecture.
• *Cast-iron buildings on Canal*—particularly no. 622, a marvel of cast-iron curlicues, pilasters, and pediments; and no. 901 (the Maison Blanche department store).

See Chapters 6, 7, 8, 10, and 11 for some other interesting edifices.

From Poydras, Convention Center Boulevard stretches out in front of the busy Ernest N. Morial Convention Center and forms the riverside of the Warehouse District. Once a scarred and ugly area of abandoned storehouses, the Warehouse District is blossoming with fine contemporary art galleries and restaurants (Emeril's, one of the hottest meal tickets in town, is in this area).

Louisiana Children's Museum

Tucked amid the art galleries on the Warehouse District's main drag, the Children's Museum offers a plethora of hands-on exhibits that mix education and safety with fun: a radio station, a miniature grocery store, and a kid-size port where children take on stevedore chores. In Toddlers Playscape wee ones can just kid around.

The museum's address is 428 Julia Street. Hours are Tuesday through Sunday from 9:30 to 4:30. Admission is $4. Phone 523-1357 for more information.

Contemporary Arts Center

The CAC is the heart and soul of the Warehouse District. It opened—appropriately enough, in an abandoned warehouse—in 1976, with the mission to provide alternative arts space for the city's burgeoning contemporary arts community. The forty thousand square feet of the renovated building contain several art galleries and two theaters that mount traveling shows as well as experimental works by local and regional playwrights. One of the nation's largest centers for the visual and performing arts, the CAC offers frequent seminars and workshops as well as dance performances and concerts.

Located at 900 Camp Street, the CAC's galleries are open Tuesday through Sunday from 11:00 to 7:00. Call

523-1216 for information about programs and admission charges.

Confederate Memorial Museum

Right across the street from the contemporary CAC scene is a century-old museum (dedicated in 1891) that holds memorabilia pertaining to the Confederate States of America. Civil War buffs will enjoy the ancient weaponry (including the first hand grenade used on a battlefield); a portion of Robert E. Lee's campaign silver service; the boots, spurs, and mess kit of one of Colonel Mosby's Raiders; bloodied flags and uniforms; and a large collection of Jefferson Davis' personal effects, donated to the museum by his widow. A good selection of Civil War books and maps can be found in the gift shop.

The museum, which is at 929 Camp Street, is open Monday through Saturday from 10:00 to 4:00. Admission is $3. Phone 523-4522 for more information.

CULTURE

The CBD has something to offer to those with a cultural bent.

- *Gallery Row (Julia Street in the Warehouse District)*
- *Contemporary Arts Center (900 Camp)*
- *Virlane Collection (K & B Plaza, 1055 St. Charles)*

See Chapters 4, 8, and 11 for other cultural treats.

Lee Circle

At the traffic circle where St. Charles and Howard Avenues collide, a sixteen-foot statue of Confederate leader Robert E. Lee stands stalwartly atop a sixty-foot granite shaft. When Lee died in 1870, the war had been over for five years and Southern states had been dismantled and divided into five military districts. Louisiana suffered under Reconstruction until 1877, and fund-raising for the tribute to Lee was a long process; the statue, sculpted by New Yorker Alexander Doyle, was finally dedicated in 1884. Present among the fifteen thousand spectators were Lee's daughters, Jefferson Davis, and New Orleans' own Creole general Pierre Gustav Toutant Beauregard.

The Virlane Collection of contemporary sculptures is displayed in an indoor/outdoor gallery at the K & B corporate headquarters across St. Charles Avenue from Lee Circle. Among the featured artists is the late Isamu Noguchi, who was commissioned in 1962 to sculpt *The Mississippi*, which stands on the plaza. National and international artists are represented in the collection.

At 1055 St. Charles, the plaza is open daily, twenty-four hours, and the lobby gallery is open Monday through Friday from 8:30 to 4:30. There is no admission charge.

St. Patrick's Cathedral

As you backtrack to Camp Street and head toward Canal, you'll see the soaring Gothic structure that served the Irish Catholics when the city was divided into three separate municipalities. To the Americans flooding into New Orleans it seemed that in St. Louis Cathedral God spoke only in French; they wanted their own house of worship. The cornerstone for the church was laid on June 1, 1838. Designed by architects James and Charles Dakin along the lines of York Minster Cathedral in England, the church was later completed by the estimable James Gallier, Sr. The elaborate interior, with its vaulted, ribbed ceilings, is Gallier's work, as is the altar; the dramatic murals over the altar were painted in 1840 by Leon Pomarade. Services, which include a Latin mass, are still conducted. The cathedral, at 724 Camp Street, is also open Monday through Friday from 9:15 to 3:00 and Friday from 10:30 to 3:00. For further information call the rectory at 525-4413.

Lafayette Square

In the nineteenth century, during the two decades that the city was divided, the area around Lafayette Square was the Americans' version of the Creoles' social, religious, and government center around Place d'Armes: St. Patrick's was their church, Gallier Hall their city hall, and Lafayette Square their public square. Gallier Hall, a splendid Greek Revival structure, was designed by James Gallier, Sr., who put the finishing touches on St. Patrick's Cathedral. When the city was consolidated in 1852, Gallier Hall became city hall—an indication of the increasing American influence—and remained so until the 1950s, when government offices were moved to the Civic Center on Loyola Avenue. Gallier Hall (not open to the public) is now used for official functions; on Mardi Gras, the mayor stands on the steps and exchanges toasts with Rex, King of Carnival, in a ritual that dates to the nineteenth century.

Louisiana Superdome

A left turn from Lafayette Square onto Poydras Street will take you up to the stupendous Superdome, a very large place indeed. Beneath its dome—680 feet in diameter—the NFL New Orleans Saints play their home games, as does the Green Wave of Tulane University. The Sugar Bowl shoot-out takes place here each New Year's Day, and the Bayou Classic is a Thanksgiving grudge match between Grambling and Southern Universities. New Orleans has hosted the Super Bowl more times than any other city, and will do so again for the 1997 face-off. Movable stands in the Dome can be shuffled like a deck of cards to accommodate the Ringling Bros. circus, Mardi Gras balls, conventions, trade shows, and big-ticket concerts.

The Dome is at 1500 Sugar Bowl Drive (which parallels Poydras). Guided tours are conducted daily. For information call 587-3810.

Church of the Immaculate Conception

Usually referred to as the Jesuit Church, this onion-domed building seems drastically out of place amid the CBD's skyscrapers. The present-day church, erected in 1930, is almost an exact replica of the church that stood on this site in 1857. That original building was demolished in 1926, having sustained structural damage due to the weight of its own ironwork and to the construction of the adjacent Père Marquette building. Moorish and Arabian in flavor, today's church contains the cast-iron pews and gilt bronze altar from the original. The altar, designed by New Orleans architect James Freret and made in France, won top honors at the 1867–68 Paris Exposition. The statue of the Virgin Mary above the altar was also made in France and meant for the Tuileries in Paris. The 1848 French Revolution threw a monkey wrench into that plan; the statue was purchased eventually by the New Orleans congregation.

Chapter Six
♦♦♦♦♦♦♦♦♦♦
On the Waterways

THERE IS something magical, mystical, and almost irresistible about the Mississippi. Mark Twain's romantic descriptions of his favorite river almost make the mighty waterway begin to flow before your very eyes. He called the great frilly riverboats that plied its waters "wedding cakes without the complications."

The ancient name for New Orleans was Isle d'Orléans, and the city is indeed surrounded by waterways. It is not only Old Man River that makes himself at home here: Lake Pontchartrain forms a forty-mile watery carpet to the north, and in the outlying areas swamps and bayous creep out beneath lacy canopies of Spanish moss. A whole slew of swamp and bayou tours nose out into the secluded sloughs. (The area code for all phone numbers is 504.)

You won't see a single sailboat or water ski on the Mississippi—at least not anywhere along the fifteen-mile Port of New Orleans. Pleasure craft are not allowed; the nation's second-largest port is restricted to commercial vessels—-freighters, cargo ships, tugboats, and, of course, the sightseeing vessels that happily combine business with pleasure.

Sightseeing cruises aboard replicas of fancy Victorian-style paddle-wheelers are among the most popular of the city's many attractions. The boats come all gussied up in nineteenth-century gingerbread trim, polished brass, glittering chandeliers—and such twentieth-century comforts as air-conditioning. The New Orleans Steamboat Company (586-8777 or 800/233-BOAT) operates the *Steamboat Natchez*, the *Cotton Blossom*, and the *John James Audubon*, all of which depart from the Toulouse Street Wharf behind the Jax Brewery in the French Quarter—a stone's throw from the 1812 parking place of the *New Orleans*, the first steamboat to successfully navigate downriver. New Orleans Tours/Paddlewheels (524-0814) churns up the Big Muddy with its *Creole Queen*, which takes on passengers at the International Cruise Ship Terminal at Poydras Street Dock, and the *Cajun Queen*, which boards at the aquarium.

If you're anywhere near the Toulouse Street Wharf any day at 11:00 A.M. or 1:45 P.M., you can't possibly miss the warbling calliope of the sixteen-hundred-passenger, four-decker *Steamboat Natchez*; the calliope does loud, rollicking concerts before each of the boat's narrated cruises. You can't help but giggle while you listen to the off-key renditions of "Red, Red Robin," "Toot, Toot, Tootsie," and other old-time favorites. And if you're like a lot of visitors, you won't be able to resist going up the gangplank and taking a two-hour tool around the harbor ($14.75). Passengers are invited to go below and see the working of the steam engine. At night the *Natchez* does dixieland and dinner cruises (see Chapter 16).

The colorful little *Cotton Blossom* gets her bright red paddle turning every day at noon for a three-hour discovery cruise downriver ($15). A naturalist from the Louisi-

---

ARCHITECTURAL GEM

Architecture lovers should map out this sight
for any waterway touring.

♦ *Doullut   Steamboat   House*—Cruising
downriver, you'll pass the frilly turn-of-the-
century home of a riverboat captain whose
career inspired the design of his house.
Once you've glimpsed it, you may want to
take a tour. (Call 279-6483 or 271-6391.)

See Chapters 6, 7, 8, 10, and 11 for more
gems.

---

ana Science and Nature Center is on board for talks and
demonstrations pertaining to Louisiana's colorful history
and rapidly vanishing wetlands. Passengers disembark at
the Chalmette Battlefield, where Andy Jackson fit the Brits
in 1815. The Chalmette visitors' center of the Jean Lafitte
National Historical Park Service runs multimedia presen-
tations, and park rangers answer questions about the
battle. The pretty three-decker *Creole Queen* also does
daily three-hour cruises to the Chalmette Battlefield
($13). The cruises differ in that the *Cotton Blossom*
focuses on ecology; the *Creole Queen* offers a larger,
prettier boat, with evening dinner/jazz cruises (see Chapter 16).

The *Creole Queen*'s sister ship, the *Cajun Queen*, does
ninety-minute river cruises for $10 and offers a combi-
nation aquarium tour and riverboat cruise for $17. The
Cajun Queen's biggest splash, however, is its Christmas
Eve bonfire cruise into the river parishes. In an age-old
Cajun tradition, on Christmas Eve huge bonfires on both

sides of the river are torched to light the way for Papa Noël. The boat sidles up to the levee and shines search-lights on the shore so you can get a good look at all the festivities. (The bonfires, incidentally, are not just piles of sticks: They're made of wood, of course, but fashioned into cottages, canoes, fire trucks—all manner of different sizes and shapes.) In the days leading up to Christmas Eve there are *fais-do-dos* (Cajun dances) in the towns and villages along the river. Gray Line (587-0861) does tours that take in the building of the bonfires and some of the festivities ($45).

The *John James Audubon*—smaller and less elaborate than her sisters—makes four cruises daily between the Aquarium of the Americas and the riverboat landing at the Audubon Zoo. Several different options are available, ranging from a one-way cruise ($9.50), to a round-trip cruise-and-zoo ($17.75), to the $25.50 round-trip cruise/aquarium/zoo. Many people opt to take the St. Charles Streetcar to the zoo and make the return downriver on a cooling cruise. The *John James Audubon* also does occa-sional dinner/jazz evening outings, and most of the boats

---

NATURAL NEW ORLEANS

Those who enjoy seeing or learning about the great outdoors will want to catch this attraction.

◆ "Discovery Cruise"—*The Cotton Blossom* noses into the bayous with a narrating nat-uralist aboard.

See Chapters 5, 7, 8, 10, and 11 for other natural highs.

usually do champagne/dinner/dancing cruises on New Year's Eve for around $100 per couple.

Come 1995 those boats will be in serious competition with a veritable flotilla of casinos. "Gambling riverboats" have long been in operation upriver, but only as recently as 1991 did Louisiana's Riverboat Gaming Commission approve such vessels. (At press time licensing of the floating casinos was picking up steam.) The first of the floating casinos did not embark on the Mississippi but on Lake Pontchartrain: The 295-foot triple-decker stern-wheeler *Star Casino* docks at a brand new 31,000-square-foot terminal adjacent to the lake's South Shore Marina. The boat itself, which began operation in late 1993, has 21,000 square feet of space and 760 slot machines, thirty blackjack tables, six craps tables, and three roulette tables.

As for high rolling on the Mississippi, the first river casino is the *Queen of New Orleans*, a 245-foot boat jointly owned by the Hilton New Orleans Corporation and New Orleans Paddlewheels, Inc. The *Queen* puts in at the Poydras Street Wharf. At least two other riverboats will gambol on the river and dock at New Orleans ports —but as of press time things were more up in the air than down on the water.

New Orleans is home port for the Delta Queen Steamboat Company (30 Robin Street Wharf, New Orleans, LA 70130-1890; 586-0631 or 800/543-1949). Traveling from northern ports—Pittsburgh, Cincinnati, and river cities along the way—you can arrive in New Orleans in fine style aboard the quaint *Delta Queen*—a floating National Historic Landmark—or her glitzy sister, the *Mississippi Queen*; they're the only two overnight steamboats in the nation. They'll be joined in 1995 by the *American Queen*, the third boat to fly the company's flag. The boat you choose depends upon your personal taste: The *Delta Queen* is small, quaint, and historic; the *Mis-*

sissippi Queen, built in 1976, is twice as large and offers luxuries such as a whirlpool, sauna, and movies. Both boats offer a wide variety of cruises with stays ranging from three nights to twelve.

Chapter Seven
♦♦♦♦♦♦♦♦♦♦♦♦

Rambling on the St. Charles Streetcar

S T. CHARLES AVENUE stretches upriver from Canal in the CBD through the Garden District, the university section, and uptown. The avenue offers little in the way of scenic beauty until it reaches the stretch that begins at Jackson Avenue, the downriver border of the Garden District. Upriver of Jackson, the branches of huge live oak trees drape over the avenue and the street is lined with one palatial mansion after the other. When you board the St. Charles Streetcar, be prepared for a lot of rubbernecking along the route. (And I'll let you in on a secret. You get the best views by standing and looking out the rear window of the car because the rear becomes the front when the car reverses direction—the window is broad so the driver can see clearly. Your panoramic view will be not of what's ahead but of what you've just passed. It's a little like the old-fashioned worry bird, who didn't care where he was going but worried about where he'd been.)

The St. Charles Streetcar, born in 1835 as the New Orleans & Carrollton Railroad, connected downtown

New Orleans with the cities of Lafayette, Jefferson City, and Carrollton ("city" was perhaps a bit grandiose for these villages). In its earliest day the railroad car was drawn by mules; the line was "electrified" in 1893, and on February 1 of that year the name was changed to the St. Charles Streetcar. In 1973 the streetcar became a moving museum piece when it was placed on the National Register of Historic Places. (New Orleanians, incidentally, never say "trolley," just as they never say "median" for neutral ground.) The olive-green cars of today were designed and built in 1923–24 by the Perley A. Thomas Car Company of High Point, North Carolina. The rumble of the cars and the ting-a-ling of the bells are familiar sounds in the city.

The streetcar unloads and loads again downtown at Canal and Carondelet Streets, clangs one block along Canal's neutral ground, and then lumbers on to St. Charles Avenue. There it stays until it turns on South Carrollton Avenue at Riverbend. You can also board along the route wherever you see the numbered yellow markers planted in the neutral ground.

To get a ninety-minute round-trip overview of the upriver area, board downtown and ride all way uptown to Palmer Park. At that point, pay an additional fare and reverse the seat back so you're facing in the right direction for the trip back to Canal. But don't attempt to see all of the Garden District, Audubon Park, and the zoo in one day. The Garden District houses described in this chapter are only a few of those worth seeing, and both the park and the zoo are made for easygoing ambling.

Although you can get on and off the streetcar anywhere along the route, you'll have to pay another fare each time you board; at a dollar a pop that can add up. The most economical way to see the Garden District and uptown areas is to purchase a VisiTour pass, good for from one to three days, which allows unlimited rides on all of the RTA-operated buses and streetcars.

The Garden District is bounded by Magazine Street on the riverside and by St. Charles, Jackson, and Louisiana Avenues. In the mid-1800s, while Frenchman J. N. B. de Pouilly was designing houses for the Creoles, for the most part Yankee, Irish, and English architects built the grand, American-style mansions for the wealthy Yankees who came pouring into New Orleans between the 1830s and the early 1860s. (*Yankee* was not a bad word in these parts until The War; *damnyankee* became one word during Reconstruction.) Henry Howard, born in County Cork; James Gallier, Sr. (real name: Gallagher) of Dublin; and Samuel Jamison, from County Antrim, near Belfast, all came to New Orleans in the 1830s. They were soon followed by Englishmen Thomas K. Wharton and John Turpin and New Yorkers James Dakin and Lewis E. Reynolds. Only two New Orleans–born architects were working in the Garden District in that period: William Freret and Thomas Sully. Sully, great-nephew of the English portrait painter, Thomas Sully, designed several of the fanciful Queen Anne houses in the Garden District. The Garden District is a residential district; homes are not open to the public. Some of the interiors can be seen, however, during Spring Fiesta, which begins on the Friday following Easter.

All Aboard

Our tour begins at Sixth Street (carstop no. 17) with a look at Christ Church Cathedral (2919 St. Charles). Built in about 1887, this splendid Gothic church was designed by New York architect Lawrence B. Valk. The transom was the work of Thomas Sully, and the more than one hundred stained-glass windows were added between 1950

The Garden District

and 1970. This is the Fourth Episcopal Cathedral of New Orleans.

At 1604 Fourth Street (corner of St. Charles), the Grima House—so named for Alfred Grima, who bought and restored the delicate Italianate house in the 1890s—is believed to date from 1850 and is known for the fanciful plasterwork on its pediment.

A block toward the river on Washington Avenue, The Rink (2727 Prytania) is now a shopping mall with only a few shops. It was built in 1884 as the Crescent City Skating Rink by a Miss Hagan, who hoped to attract visitors to the World's Industrial and Cotton Centennial Exposition held that year in what is now Audubon Park.

The walls on Washington Avenue and Prytania, Sixth,

and Coliseum Streets enclose Lafayette Cemetery. The oldest tombs date from the 1830s, when this was the graveyard for the city of Lafayette. (The old cemetery was the setting for some of the scenes in Anne Rice's novel *The Witching Hour*.) As with other area cemeteries, this one is not safe to venture into alone. Just across the street from the cemetery is Commander's Palace, one of the city's finest restaurants, in a big turreted house that dates from 1883.

More Stately Mansions

The great Italianate mansion called Colonel Short's Villa (1448 Fourth, corner of Prytania) was designed by Henry Howard in 1859 for Colonel Robert Short of Kentucky. The cast-iron fence, with its intricate cornstalk motif, is a twin of the one at 915 Royal Street in the French Quarter. Howard built this house the same year he designed one of his greatest concoctions—Nottoway plantation on the Great River Road (see Chapter 10). Across the street, at 2631 Prytania, is the Sully Mansion—now a bed-and-breakfast—a delightful Queen Anne house designed around 1890 by Thomas Sully. In the same block (2605 Prytania), the Gothic Briggs-Staub House was designed in 1849 by James Gallier, Sr. for British-born Charles Briggs; the little guesthouse set back from the street is an exact copy of the main house.

Greek Revival meets Queen Anne in the Women's Opera Guild House (2504 Prytania). Built in 1858 as a home for Edward Davis, its last resident was the late Nettie Seebold, who bequeathed the house to the Opera Guild in 1955. The house is open for touring, but only for groups of twenty or more. The splendid house at 2521 Prytania is now home to Our Lady of Perpetual Help Chapel, a chapel of the Redemptorist Fathers. It was built in 1856 for Henry Lonsdale, who was born in Brooklyn, spent his childhood in England, and amassed a fortune in New Orleans as a coffee broker and gunnysack manufacturer. John Adams, born in New Jersey and raised in Ohio, came to New Orleans in 1842 and got rich quick as a wholesale grocer; the handsome Greek Revival cottage built for him is at 2423 Prytania.

On St. Charles Avenue, the Greek Revival raised cottage at no. 2524 has an uncertain history. According to some accounts it was built for Antoine Mandeville de Marigny —a son of the Creole Bernard de Marigny—and his American wife, Louise Claiborne. The tall, handsome mansion two blocks away (no. 2265) was built by James Gallier, Jr. in 1857—the same year he built his own home on Royal Street in the French Quarter. Gallier built the house on St. Charles for Miss Lavinia Dabney, who is said to have suffered financially and had to move out of her house after only a year.

One block toward the river, at 2221 Prytania, the Grinnan-Reilly House dates from 1850; it was designed by Henry Howard for cotton broker Robert Grinnan. In 1854 James Gallier, Sr. built the Greek Revival raised cottage at 2336 St. Charles for a Miss Susan Hackett.

Since 1929, the handsome Second Empire house at 2343 Prytania has been the Louise McGehee School, a very posh private school for girls. It was built in 1872 as a home for planter Bradish Johnson, who appears to have made a killing during Reconstruction. Across the street, at 2340 Prytania, Toby's Corner—built for Philadelphian Thomas Toby—is believed to be the oldest house in the Garden District. Dating from about 1838, it is a simple (though hardly small) raised cottage set in lush grounds. The majestic tree, named the Livaudais Oak, is a member in good standing of the Louisiana Live Oak Society; most members of this select group are several centuries old and have long grey beards of Spanish moss clinging to their limbs.

ARCHITECTURAL GEMS

Architecture lovers should map out these
sights for any streetcar touring.

* *Garden District standouts:*
    Louise McGehee School (2343 Prytania)
    Robinson House (1415 Third)
    Musson-Bell House (1331 Third)
    Colonel Short's Villa (1448 Fourth)
* *St. Charles Avenue standouts:*
    Sacred Heart Academy (no. 4521)
    Brown House (no. 4717)
    Milton H. Latter Memorial Library (no.
       5120)
    Tara (no. 5705)
    Wedding Cake House (no. 5809)

See Chapters 5, 6, 8, 10, and 11 for more
gems.

First Street displays a number of notable houses. The
Morris-Israel House (no. 1331) and the nearby Carroll-
Crawford House (no. 1315) were both designed in 1869
by Samuel Jamison and have identical cast-iron galleries.
The handsome mansion at no. 1239, known variously as
the Rosegate, Brevard, or Mmahat House, was built in
about 1857; it is now owned by native New Orleanian
novelist Anne Rice, who restored it and used it as the
setting for *The Witching Hour.* In the next block toward
the river, the Payne-Strachan House (no. 1134) dates from
1849 and was the home of a Kentuckian, Judge Jacob
Payne. Jefferson Davis, ex-president of the Confederacy,

and Judge Payne were longtime friends; Davis died in this house in 1889.

One of the most unusual houses in the Garden District is at 1213 Third: the Montgomery-Hero House. The bracketed house was built in 1868 for the Irishman Archibald Montgomery, president of the Crescent City Railroad. In 1853 Michel Musson had the frame Italianate house built at 1331 Third. Musson was a Creole, a New Orleans postmaster, and an uncle, by marriage, of French impressionist painter Edgar Degas. In 1872 the Mussons moved to a house on Esplanade Avenue, where Degas was a visitor. The Third Street house appears somewhat small when viewed from the front; you get the full impact by walking around to the side. The spectacular white house at 1415 Third was built toward the end of the Civil War for Walter Robinson, a banker from Virginia.

The frivolous "Swiss chalet" at 2627 Coliseum, built in the 1860s and awash with ornamentation, is certainly an Orleanian original; it seems to cry out for alps instead of oaks.

University Area

Two blocks from Coliseum, at carstop no. 16 between Fourth and Washington, you can resume your trip to Audubon Park and its zoo. From here on St. Charles is one mansion after the other. You can't possibly see all of them on one trip; even longtime residents spot treasures they'd never noticed before. One standout is The Columns (no. 3811), an 1880s concoction that was used for interior shots of the Louis Malle film *Pretty Baby* (it's been a guesthouse for a number of years). Another is the Rayne Memorial Methodist Church (no. 3900), with its tall belfry; it dates from 1875. At no. 4521, *the* Catholic school for girls is Sacred Heart Academy, begun in 1899 and completed in 1905. On the same side of the street, at no. 4717, the Brown House is a dramatic Richardsonian

Romanesque edifice. The Orleans Club (no. 5005), home of one of the city's oldest women's organizations, was built in 1868. One of the elaborate homes that can be visited is at no. 5120; the Milton H. Latter Memorial Library is a branch of the public library. Built in 1907, it was once the home of silent-screen star Marguerite Clark. Tara (no. 5705) is an exact replica of Scarlett O'Hara's home; the "real" Tara from *Gone with the Wind* was built on a Hollywood back lot, but this Tara was built in 1941 according to the set designer's plans. Keep an eye out in the next block (no. 5809) for the Wedding Cake House—all it needs is a bride and groom on the top tier.

Two of the city's universities, Loyola and Tulane, sit side by side on St. Charles, their beautifully landscaped campuses almost overlapping. Loyola's U-shaped Gothic-*cum*-Tudor complex, built by the Jesuits in 1911, occupies the 6300 block; majestic Holy Name of Jesus Church was built in 1914. Tulane University, founded in 1834 as the University of New Orleans in the CBD—University Place is named for it—was privately endowed in 1884 by Paul Tulane. It has been in its present location since the late 1880s and is renowned for its schools of law and medicine.

Audubon Park and Zoo

Directly across the street from the universities, Audubon Park provides a 380-acre urban oasis. The World's Industrial and Cotton Centennial Exposition of 1884–85 was on this site, its main building covering the present eighteen-hole golf course. Long before that it was the plantation of Etienne de Bore, the first mayor of New Orleans after the Louisiana Purchase. De Bore might be called the patron saint of dentists: In 1795 he was the first person to figure out how to granulate sugar for commercial purchase—thus paving the way for countless Porsches and BMWs.

Named for naturalist John James Audubon, whose statue stands in a grove of trees, Audubon Park was designed in part by the famous Frederick Law Olmsted, whose green thumb was responsible for many of the nation's landscaped parks. He had a lot of help from Mother Nature in New Orleans: Audubon Park is naturally endowed with subtropical greenery and stately live oak trees dressed in frilly Spanish moss. In addition to lush golf links, the park has a jogging track with eighteen exercise stations, lagoons to laze beside, miles of hiking and biking trails, tennis courts, and the Cascade Stable, where you can sign on for an hour-long guided trail ride through the park.

Audubon Zoo spreads over fifty-eight acres between the park and the river. To reach it, you can stroll through the park—about a half-hour walk—or take the free shuttle that leaves every fifteen minutes from the streetcar stop. (The zoo is also accessible via the riverboat *John James Audubon*, which docks at the levee entrance, and the Magazine Street bus, which lets you off right at the front entrance.) Some fifteen hundred exotic beasts roam the zoo in such naturalistic habitats as an African Savannah, the Asian Domain, Australia, Grasslands of the World, and the Louisiana Swamp Exhibit (where alligators laze on bayous below the wooden deck and signs somewhat unnecessarily warn people not to sit on or drop anything over the rail). The zoo has a reptile building, a World of Primates, and a sea lion exhibit, wherein there is joyous barking and splashing at feeding time. The Mombasa Railroad, a miniature tram, ambles through six of the regions, and wooden walkways string through the whole complex.

The zoo, one of the nation's five best and a wonderful outing, is at 6500 Magazine Street. It's open Monday to Friday from 9:30 to 5:00 and Saturday and Sunday from 9:30 to 6:00. Admission is $7.75. Phone 861-2537 for more information.

Chapter Eight
◆◆◆◆◆◆◆◆◆◆◆◆

Mid-City and the Lakefront

SPRAWLING OVER considerable acreage between downtown and Lake Pontchartrain, the bowl-shaped Mid-City area, formerly swamps and eighteenth-century plantations, is now primarily residential. It was here, near City Park, that Jean-Baptiste Le Moyne, Sieur de Bienville, first established a small, rather tentative settlement at approximately the location of Encampment Street. Bayou Road, which still exists, was the ancient Indian trail that led from the bayou Bienville christened St. John to the river. In the late eighteenth century Baron de Carondelet's canal connected the French Quarter with Bayou St. John, and thence to the lake. Crowded now with houses and businesses and laced with busy thoroughfares, it's hard to imagine how it may have appeared to the first French settlers: a major mess, most likely, and a wet and soggy one at that.

Wheels are an absolute necessity for tooling around Mid-City and Lakeshore Drive. Don't expect to cover the whole of this area in just one day; you will need several trips to fully take in everything City Park alone has to offer. The area code is 504.

Longue Vue House and Gardens

Forty-three blocks from the French Quarter, just off Metairie Road, the heiress to the Sears fortune, Edith Rosenwald Stern, lived in this forty-five-room mansion with her husband, wealthy cotton broker and philanthropist Edgar Bloom Stern. Modeled after one of the great English manor houses, Longue Vue is in a country setting on the border of Orleans and Jefferson parishes. Eight acres of meticulously manicured gardens surround the Greek Revival mansion, among them a Portuguese canal garden, a Louisiana native garden, and a Spanish court styled after the fourteenth-century Generalife Gardens in the Alhambra. The interior of the 1930s mansion—which has been open to the public ever since the Sterns' death—is resplendent with ornate cornices and millwork, elegantly dressed full-length windows, and handsome wall coverings. The house is furnished with the Sterns' European, American, and Oriental antiques and *objets d'art.*

Longue Vue is at 7 Bamboo Road. Concerts and other special events are sometimes held, but regular touring hours are Monday through Saturday from 10:00 to 4:30 (last tour at 3:45) and Sunday from 1:00 to 5:00 (last tour at 4:15). Admission is $6. For directions or additional information, call 488-5488.

Metairie Cemetery

The city's largest, most elaborate, and most photogenic cemetery is a few minutes away from Longue Vue via Metairie Road. The oval shape of the 150-acre drive-through graveyard stems from its having been a thriving racetrack in the 1850s. One old legend has it that a gent named Charles T. Howard was denied entrance to the track's exclusive Jockey Club, a snub that prompted him to declare he'd buy the place and turn it into a graveyard. It has been a cemetery since 1872, but . . . well, Orleanians love their legends of pirates and voodoo queens and cemeteries. It's a beautiful place in which to be planted, landscaped as it is with gardens, live oaks, lagoons, and . . . tombs. Many of the more than seven thousand monumental monuments, mausoleums, and society tombs are clearly visible from I-10, which almost sideswipes the cemetery. Among the late-lamented in Metairie are governors and mayors, kings and queens of Carnival, and Josie Arlington, the famed madam of Storyville. For four years after his death in 1889, Jefferson Davis was buried in the tomb of the Army of Northern Virginia, atop which stands an equestrian statue of Confederate general Albert Sidney Johnston. Davis' body lay in state in Gallier Hall (then City Hall), and his funeral was one of the largest the city has ever seen; it lasted four hours

---

ARCHITECTURAL GEMS

Architecture lovers should map out these sights for any Mid-City touring.

- *Longue Vue House and Gardens (7 Bamboo)*
- *Pitot House (1440 Moss)*
- *Metairie Cemetery*—tombs, temples, statuary, and mausoleums.

See Chapters 5, 6, 7, 10, and 11 for more gems.

and was attended by more than a hundred thousand mourners. The remains of the one and only president of the Confederate States of America were later moved to Richmond.

City Park

On the other side of I-10, Metairie Road becomes City Park Avenue, so named because it streaks along the southern border of City Park. (Outside of the downtown area it's easier to keep track of cardinal directions.) City Park occupies part of a land grant that France awarded to François Hery in 1718, the year la Nouvelle Orléans was founded. In 1854, after the land had passed through several different owners, the fourth district court declared this to be a public park; at fifteen hundred luxuriant acres, it is one of the nation's largest urban parks. It is well endowed with ancient live oak trees, several of which are charter members of the Louisiana Live Oak Society. The John McDonogh, an old fellow named for New Orleans' great benefactor (and one of the park's early owners), doesn't discuss his age, but it is believed to be in the neighborhood of a thousand years. (The tree is near City Park Avenue, across Metairie Bayou from the casino.)

There is much to do and to see in City Park: thirty-nine tennis courts, four 18-hole golf courses, a hundred-tee driving range, eight miles of lagoons for boating and fishing, baseball and softball diamonds, a seven-acre botanical garden, Storyland (with Mother Goose characters, storytelling, and puppet shows for the wee ones), and an amusement park that has a carousel whose fabulous flying horses date from the turn of the century. Young and old alike enjoy the P. G. T. Beauregard miniature train that travels a two-and-a-half mile scenic route.

The casino is the place to obtain fishing permits (you can't fish in the park without one), reservations for baseball or softball diamonds, and bike, canoe, and pedal-boat rentals (call the outdoors department at 483-9371). For golf information and reservations, call the main club-house (483-9397). There are fees for some attractions; for general information about the park call 482-4888.

New Orleans Museum of Art

The New Orleans Museum of Art is at the end of Lelong Avenue, a lovely tree-shaded street at City Park and Esplanade Avenues (an impressive equestrian statue of General P. G. T. Beauregard guards the Lelong entrance to the park). In 1993 NOMA, as it is called locally, completed a $23 million expansion of the original 1911 building that doubled floor space to 130,850 square feet, added forty-six new galleries, and allowed for the exhibition of five thousand artworks. The museum's collection is valued at $200 million; the most valuable painting—a portrait of Estelle Musson, appraised at $15 million—was limned by Edgar Degas on his 1872 visit. Asian, African, and other non-Western artists, as well as seventeenth- to nineteenth-century European masters are featured, along with a section devoted to Louisiana art, a

---

CULTURE

Mid-City has something to offer to those with a cultural bent.

♦ *New Orleans Museum of Art (Lelong Drive, City Park)*

See Chapters 4, 5, and 11 for other cultural treats.

---

contemporary art gallery, a six thousand-piece photography collection, and a gallery of changing exhibits.

Located on Lelong Avenue, NOMA is open daily (except Monday) from 10:00 to 5:00. Admission is $6; Louisiana residents with proper IDs are admitted free on Thursday mornings. For further information phone 488-2631.

Pitot House

Bayou St. John lolls alongside City Park's eastern border and drifts in a southwesterly direction. Moss Street, which sweeps along the shores of the bayou, has some lovely homes. One such is the Pitot House, built in the late eighteenth century in a style typical of the West Indies houses built by this area's first settlers. Of brick-between-posts construction, wrapped in verandahs and topped by a double-pitched roof, the house was purchased in 1810 by James Pitot (locals make it rhyme with teapot), who replaced Etienne de Bore as mayor in 1805. Headquarters now of the Louisiana Landmark Society, which meticulously restored it, the house contains authentic period furnishings. This is a grand place to see how the early French settlers lived—bearing in mind that when the house was built this was still mushy swamplands.

The Pitot House, at 1440 Moss Street, is open Wednesday through Saturday from 10:00 to 3:00. Admission is $3. Phone 482-0312 for more information.

New Orleans Fair Grounds

To the east of City Park, the Fair Grounds has live thoroughbred racing November through April, every Wednesday through Sunday (post time is 1:30). The third-oldest racetrack in the nation, it was established in 1872 —the same year, incidentally, that another nearby track was buried and born again as Metairie Cemetery—and was the first to have a mechanical starting gate. General admission is one dollar; the clubhouse ($4) has an eighteen-hundred-seat restaurant that serves a Cajun buffet Saturday and Sunday. On the third level, the President's Crescent City Jockey Club is a posh suite that must be reserved in advance; it has a private-access elevator, a hostess, complimentary champagne, two television monitors, and unsurpassed views. The infield of the Fair Grounds is also the main stomping grounds for the annual New Orleans Jazz and Heritage Festival, which takes place in the late spring (see Chapter 9).

Louisiana Nature and Science Center

The eighty-six-acre facility of the Louisiana Nature and Science Center in eastern New Orleans gives city folks a look at the state's wetlands and forests. The indoor/outdoor complex includes a teaching greenhouse; a sixty-six-seat planetarium, which has regularly scheduled explorations of the universe; a Discovery Loft with hands-on exhibits; and an interpretive center with exhibits that pertain to our relationship with the universe. A large window in the interpretive center overlooks a wildlife garden where squirrels, rabbits, birds, and other critters come to feed and frolic. The three nature trails range from a three-quarter-mile wheelchair-accessible trail to a mile-and-a-quarter trail.

The center is in Joe W. Brown Memorial Park. To reach it, take I-10 east to Read Boulevard (exit 244) and turn right; after the third traffic light you'll come to Nature Center Boulevard, which will take you to the entrance. The center is open Tuesday to Friday from 9:00 to 5:00, Saturday from 10:00 to 5:00, and Sunday from noon to 5:00. Admission is $4. Phone 246-5672 for more information.

NATURAL NEW ORLEANS

Those who enjoy seeing or learning about the great outdoors will want to catch these Mid-City attractions.

♦ *City Park*
♦ *Lakeshore Drive and Lake Pontchartrain*
♦ *Louisiana Nature and Science Center*

See Chapters 5, 6, 7, 10, and 11 for other natural highs.

Lakeshore Drive

As the name suggests, scenic Lakeshore Drive breezes along the shores of Lake Pontchartrain. The large, shallow lake—forty miles long and twenty-four miles wide—is the favorite summertime playground for New Orleanians. There are colorful marinas on the lakefront, and plenty of grassy-green spaces for picnicking or just lazing. On weekends and late summer afternoons sailboats move gracefully across the waters.

The sailboats have been joined by another kind of boat: the 295-foot triple-decker stern-wheeler *Star Casino*. The high-rolling riverboat—or lakeboat, if you will—began operating in late 1993, from a new, 31,000-square-foot terminal adjacent to the lake's South Shore Marina. The boat boasts 760 slot machines, thirty blackjack tables, six craps tables, and three roulette tables. Not all New Orleanians are thrilled with the prospect of traffic jams and crowds cluttering up their peaceful recreation area.

From the South Shore Marina, the drive stretches westward along the lake to West End Park. At Franklin Avenue you'll pass the Kiefer UNO Lakefront Arena, part of the

University of New Orleans and one of the venues for sports events and top name entertainers. After you pass Marconi Drive, you'll see on your left the Mardi Gras Fountain. Due to a shortage of city funds, the fountain is not always operational; when it is functioning, the leaping waters are illuminated with the purple, gold, and green colors of Carnival. The sixty-foot fountain is surrounded by plaques of all of the Mardi Gras krewes, or private clubs, both past and present. This area also abounds with parking bays and grassy picnic areas.

Lakeshore Drive ends at West End Park, one of the city's prettiest, most peaceful places, and home to the Orleans Marina and the Southern Yacht Club. Established in 1849, the yacht club is the nation's second oldest. Park and stroll around the marina and boulevard, which has huge, moss-draped live oak trees. West End Park also abounds with seafood restaurants.

To reach the Lake Pontchartrain Causeway, drive down Pontchartrain Boulevard, head east on I-10, and then take a right on Causeway Boulevard. At the entrance to the causeway, park and stroll over to the bird-watching area just under it. (The area is well marked, and you'll see crowds of people headed there in the early evening.) Every night during July—usually late in the month—some two hundred thousand purple martins fly to their sleeping berths beneath the bridge. The lake and the sunset are spectacularly beautiful, and it's fascinating to watch the birds jockeying for position. Plan to show up before 6:30; the birds turn in pretty early, and it's usually all over by 7:00.

Chapter Nine
◆◆◆◆◆◆◆◆◆◆

Mardi Gras and Other Madness

I F YOU'VE NEVER been to Mardi Gras, one of the first things you should know is that it is *not* mandatory to expose a part of your anatomy while standing on a Bourbon Street balcony. Oh, yes, there will be those who will try to convince you that this is an age-old Mardi Gras tradition. And you may even feel some amount of peer pressure when you see bared this, that, and those on various balconies. (Truth to tell, the baring is not necessarily confined to balconies.) No wonder they call Mardi Gras the greatest free show on earth.

Carnival and Mardi Gras

Carnival season begins on January 6, otherwise known as Twelfth Night and the Feast of the Epiphany. On that day, one of the St. Charles streetcars is commandeered by a group called the Phunny Phorty Phellows—accompanied by dixieland bands and a phew equally phunny phemales —who have a fine old time jazzing up and down the avenue and getting Carnival season started with the proper spirit(s).

Also on Twelfth Night, bakeries all over town start selling king cakes—wreath-shaped coffee cakes frosted with the Mardi Gras colors of gold, green, and purple. Hidden within each cake is a plastic baby or, sometimes, a bean. Traditionally, the person who gets the slice that contains baby or bean has to buy the next king cake or host the next king cake party. During Carnival season the Crescent City has more king cakes than the entire South has black-eyed peas.

Carnival parades begin rolling soon after January 6, but the really big blowout heats up in the last two weeks of the season. (Carnival and Mardi Gras, incidentally, are not synonymous. Mardi Gras is the culmination of the Carnival season. Technically, Mardi Gras—French for Shrove Tuesday, or Fat Tuesday—is the final day of the Carnival season. In New Orleans the term also refers to the last two weeks of the season.) Things reach a fever pitch the final ten days before Fat Tuesday, and the weekend before the big day is total madness, with parades day and night and nonstop partying all over town.

The parades and Carnival balls are staged by private clubs or organizations called "krewes"—a term created and adopted in 1857 by the Mystick Krewe of Comus, the first organized club. The clubs are neither supported nor subsidized by the city. Members' dues pay for the costs of parading, including the souvenirs—called "throws"—that are tossed to the throngs along the parade routes. A wide variety of throws are thrown—toy footballs, bikinis, go-cups, Frisbees, candy—but among the most popular are beads and doubloons. Beads—cheap, plastic, and wildly coveted—are worn like badges of honor; you can identify the veteran parade-goers by the number of beads they wear. Doubloons—aluminum "coins" emblazoned with the krewe emblem—shower over the parade routes like snowflakes swirling around Wisconsin in winter.

Although the more aggressive parade-watchers will go to great lengths to prevent someone else from snagging an object of desire (some veterans bring stepladders and butterfly nets, the better to bag beads and bikinis), participants in the melee can also be remarkably generous. The person who has just risked life and limb to retrieve a few beads will often hand them over to some poor beadless wretch who obviously couldn't catch a cold—and will do so with a smile and a "Happy Mardi Gras."

Several of the parades feature double-decker animated and illuminated floats; all have a number of marching bands blaring out the schmaltzy Mardi Gras theme song, "If Ever I Cease to Love." The number of floats in a parade ranges from twelve to thirty-five. The two largest clubs—Endymion and Bacchus—each have twenty-seven fantastically elaborate floats with riders outfitted in billowing plumes, feathers, and glittery sequins. The masked float riders are krewe members. Duded out in colorful costumes of satins and sequins, they have a splendid time belting out beads and things—in the case of Zulu, the souvenirs include the prized gilded coconuts and spears.

The day before Mardi Gras—called Lundi Gras, or Fat Monday—the city throws a big masked ball, free to the public, at Spanish Plaza, featuring live music by top names (often the Neville Brothers or Dr. John), plenty of fireworks, and the first appearance of Rex, King of Carnival. The mayor is on hand to greet His Majesty, who arrives on a riverboat and makes a brief address. The possibility does exist—although no data supports this supposition—that some people actually get some sleep on the eve of Mardi Gras.

Things get going pretty early Mardi Gras morn. Among the first groups to hit the streets are the walking clubs. Pete Fountain's Half-Fast Walking Club is the best

MARDI GRAS SURVIVAL GUIDE

- Pick up a copy of Arthur Hardy's *Mardi Gras Guide*.
- Ladies: It is not mandatory for you to bare your breasts for the male float riders (but you'll collect a *lot* of beads if you do). You'll also need shoulders on which to sit, the better to reach riders on double-decker floats.
- During the frenzy of a parade never reach out a bare hand to pick up doubloons or beads from the pavement. Clamp your foot on them first, both to establish possession and to avoid broken limbs.
- It is wise to keep an eye peeled for flying spears during the parade of the Zulu Social Aid and Pleasure Club on Fat Tuesday.
- Police frown on folks dangling from lampposts and tree limbs (the better to see the parades).
- Remember: New Orleanians are not passive parade-watchers. They participate by screaming at the top of their lungs, and will throw body blocks in order to capture coveted souvenirs.

known, but the Jefferson City Buzzards have been around for ages. They don't actually "march," but they do straggle well: They make frequent stops in bars along the way. Other early risers are the Mardi Gras Indians, clad in some of Carnival's most opulent costumes, who participate in ancient traditions as they parade on the fringes of the CBD. The first full-scale parade of the day is Zulu, which is always scheduled to appear on Canal Street at 8:30 and never gets there before 10:30 or so. (Schedules are rarely adhered to during Mardi Gras.) The appearance of Rex is heralded by the monarch's masked, white-plumed captain, who rides in on a white stallion and is accompanied by thirty-three mounted lieutenants in splendid costumes. Rex is always portrayed by a civic leader, his queen by a debutante. (All of the krewes have a king, queen, captain, and royal court.)

In 1872 it was the Rex organization that established most of the traditions of Carnival. In that year, when Comus, a night parade, was the only Mardi Gras parade, the grand duke Alexis Romanov of Russia was visiting New Orleans during carnival season. To stage a day parade in the proper regal spirit, a fraternal organization put together a day parade replete with a Rex (the Latin name for king), so called in honor of the royal visitor. The paraders went back and forth in front of the reviewing stand, wearing what are now the traditional colors of green, purple, and gold, and accompanied by bands that blared "If Ever I Cease to Love." The song, from a popular stage show of the time, was sung by a Miss Lydia Thompson. According to legend, the grand duke had been smitten with Miss Lydia when he saw her perform in New York, and with her show scheduled to open in New Orleans, he decided it would be most enjoyable to visit the Crescent City.

Almost all of the downtown parades come down St. Charles Avenue, turn on Canal, then blare through the CBD. The balconies on Bourbon Street, too, are jammed with very exuberant and not entirely sober folk who toss beads to the sardines down below and comport themselves quite differently, it is hoped, from the way they behave back home. All of the local television stations (and, at times, MTV and even the BBC) do live coverage of Bourbon on Mardi Gras, and the camera people have to exercise extreme caution in panning the revelers. But take heart: There are also thousands of properly attired people—walking pencils, trash cans, and fire hydrants, not to mention harem girls, Marie Antoinettes, Charlie Browns, and Napoleons.

Mardi Gras is officially over at midnight on Fat Tuesday, when Ash Wednesday begins. Mounted police start at Canal and slowly work their way along Bourbon, announcing through bullhorns, "Mardi Gras is over. Everybody go home. Mardi Gras is over." After the massive cleanup, the success of Mardi Gras is measured in tons of trash.

Although the date of Mardi Gras varies each year, it always falls forty days before Easter, not counting Sundays; thus it can be any time from early March to late February. Future Fat Tuesdays will be on February 28, 1995; February 20, 1996; and February 11, 1997.

Early Spring Flings

The Black Heritage Festival in mid-March, which follows hard on the heels of Mardi Gras, offers various events at the Louisiana State Museum, Riverwalk, and the Audubon Zoo. The focus is on the contributions of African-Americans to Louisiana's rich cultural gumbo.

Lent is interrupted twice during March for celebrations and/or observations, the first being St. Patrick's Day, which this city celebrates with no fewer than three parades. Immediately following the Irish parades, the Italians roll out their St. Joseph's Day parade—the only parade other than Mardi Gras at which the Mardi Gras Indians appear. New Orleans just can't get enough of parades: There is even an Irish-Italian one. It is not uncommon for New Orleanians to whip up a brass band

MARCH EVENTS FOR THE LITERATI

◆ The annual New Orleans Writers Conference (c/o UNO Metro College Conference Services, ED 122, New Orleans, LA 70148; 504/286-6680) brings in nationally known editors, publishers, literary agents, and writers to address and meet with registrants from all over the globe.

◆ The Tennessee Williams New Orleans Literary Festival (c/o UNO Metro College Conference Services, ED 122, New Orleans, 70148; 504/286-6680) at the University of New Orleans salutes the prize-winning playwright with plays, parties, and seminars.

◆ The Faulkner Society (624 Pirate's Alley, New Orleans, 70116; 504/524-2940) has an annual birthday party for William Faulkner, celebrating the author with readings, symposia, and festivities.

and a float for no other reason than that parading is a nifty thing to do.

On the Friday night following Easter, horsedrawn carriages overflowing with belles in crinolines, and gents in frock coats clip-clop through the French Quarter streets in one of the loveliest of the many parades—"A Night in Old New Orleans," which ushers in Spring Fiesta. The week-long fiesta features open houses in some of the city's most elegant homes as well as candlelit patio and courtyard tours. By this time the city has blossomed out in all its subtropical finery, making Spring Fiesta an excellent time to visit.

The French Quarter Festival, usually held on the second weekend in April, gets bigger every year. The festival lines the streets of the Quarter, Jackson Square, and the French Market with food booths and bandstands, and lets 'er rip. And guess what: The festival kicks off with a big parade.

Jazz Fest

Second in size to Mardi Gras is the internationally acclaimed New Orleans Jazz and Heritage Festival, known to its many fans as Jazz Fest. The Jazz Fest crowd is entirely different from the Mardi Gras revelers. Jazz Fest people are music worshipers who come to town to revel in the tones of Wynton Marsalis, the Neville Brothers, Irma Thomas, and Harry Connick, Jr., to name just the homegrown favorites. More than four thousand renowned musicians and some three hundred thousand fans swarm into the city for the ten-day affair, which begins on the last weekend in April and stretches over to the first weekend in May. During the weekends, the big doings are at the New Orleans Fair Grounds, where food, crafts, and music tents dot the racetrack's infield. During the week, music sizzles and pops—all night, all over town, and out on the river. Jazz Fest is a very big deal indeed; it draws musicians and music lovers from Australia, Amsterdam, England, Scandinavia—all over the globe.

From Tomatoes to Creole Christmas

June, another big festival month, kicks off with the Great French Market Tomato Festival. You've scarcely recovered from tomato tastings when it's time for the Reggae Riddums Festival, which showcases the world's best reggae, calypso, and soca musicians, as well as African and Caribbean arts, crafts, food, and drink. There's not much time to rest before late June's Carnaval Latino, the Gulf South's largest, most elaborate celebration of Hispanic heritage and culture, featuring—ahem—a parade. Go 4th on the River, the Crescent City's big Fourth of July celebration, culminates with blazing fireworks displays over Old Man River.

Early September sees the New Orleans Saints kick off the NFL season in the Louisiana Superdome. October begins with the Swamp Festival, whose food, music, and crafts shows salute Louisiana's unique Cajun culture. The Swamp Festival flows right into the Gumbo Festival, a three-day celebration of one of South Louisiana's favorite foods. The Italians are out in force again for the annual Columbus Day parade and festivities; Piazza d'Italia is transformed into one big block party. And in a city in which the words *costume* and *mask* are verbs, Halloween is becoming more akin to Mardi Gras. The French Quarter fair crawls with party-bound folk gotten up as vampires and witches (a moonlight witches' run helps to get things off the ground).

Beginning in late November and continuing until January 3, the Celebration in the Oaks is a dazzling nightly affair in which City Park's majestic live oaks wink and twinkle with Christmas lights. It is a beautiful sight to behold, whether you're driving by in your car, strolling through, or riding on the miniature train.

The month of December is dedicated to A Creole Christmas, during which the city celebrates the season in nineteenth-century style. Papa Noël parades into town, historic house museums are decorated in period finery, and the slate of activities includes tree lightings, Christmas caroling, bonfire tours on the levees, displays of gingerbread houses, and tea parties for kids and their dolls. It's a family affair, and hotels offer special "Papa

Noël" reduced rates during the month. On New Year's Eve, Jackson Square is New Orleans' answer to Times Square; a huge crowd collects for the countdown and watches the ball drop from atop the Jackson Brewery. New Year's Eve in N'Awlins is a big event, made especially so because the Sugar Bowl is played in the Dome on the next night, with all the attendant hootin', hollerin', and hoopla.

And less than a week after the last dawg dies in the Dome and the lights go out in City Park, the wheel turns yet again: Bakeries all over town start to bake king cakes; purple, green, and gold buntings appear on French Quarter balconies; and krewe members loosen up their throwing arms in anticipation of heaving some more beads.

For information about any and all of the festivals and events, write to the Greater New Orleans Tourist and Convention Commission, 1520 Sugar Bowl Drive, New Orleans, LA 70112.

Chapter Ten
♦♦♦♦♦♦♦♦♦♦

Plantation Country

T HE GREAT RIVER ROAD hugs the mighty Mississippi all the way from just west of New Orleans up through St. Francisville and northward into Mississippi and beyond. The very name Great River Road conjures up images of knee-weakening scenery, and once upon a time the road was beautiful. Nowadays, sadly, much of the landscape is decorated with sprawling chemical and industrial plants, and views of the river are obstructed by the levees. However, it is wise not to knock the levees; just contemplate the alternative as you stroll atop one and marvel at the well-contained river.

Although the road itself is less than decorative, it is adorned with stately antebellum mansions, many of which have been restored and are open to the public. Almost all are on the National Register of Historic Places, and several are bed-and-breakfasts that offer a delicious peak into Old World living—with modern conveniences. Several tour companies—among them Tours by Isabelle, New Orleans Tours, and Gray Line—will run you out to plantation country, but you can also rent a car and travel

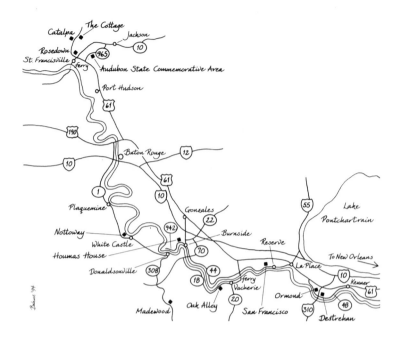

Plantation Country

along at your leisure. The New Orleans Welcome Center (529 St. Ann Street, on Jackson Square) has driving tour maps of the Great River Road as well as helpful advice (Greater New Orleans Tourist and Convention Commission, 1520 Sugar Bowl Drive, New Orleans, LA 70112; 504/566-5011).

No one can see all of the plantations in a single day and survive the experience. The nearest is twenty-two miles from New Orleans and the farthest is 116 miles from the city, in St. Francisville, north of Baton Rouge. You could spend several days exploring plantation country, overnighting at this or that B&B along the way. There are houses to see on both sides of the river, and the Great River Road travels along under several different aliases: LA 18, LA 44, and LA 48, for instance. The houses are open for guided tours every day (except major holidays). Admission fees range from $5 to $10. The area code for all phone numbers is 504.

Destrehan Plantation

The closest plantation to New Orleans is also the oldest intact one in the lower Mississippi valley. It was built in the West Indies style in 1787 by a free man of color. The wings were added in 1810, the Greek Revival embellishments in the mid-1800s. Destrehan is interesting for its age, its construction of handhewn cypress timbers, its *bousillage* (a mixture of moss and animal hair that is used for insulation), and its double-pitched dormered roof.

The house, at 9999 River Road, is open daily from 9:30 to 4:00. Phone 764-9315 for more information.

Ormond Plantation

Ormond, also a late eighteenth-century West Indies house, located about a mile west of Destrehan, was restored in the late 1980s. In addition to its interesting architecture, the house has rooms full of antiques—dolls and doll carriages, slot machines, and firearms. Ormond is a bed-and-breakfast with three rooms to let; from your second-floor gallery you can watch big freighters that look as if they're gliding along the levee.

Ormond's address is 8407 River Road. Touring hours are from 10:00 to 4:00. B&B rooms start at $125. Phone 764-8544 for more information.

San Francisco

Fans of the late novelist Frances Parkinson Keyes will be interested to know that this house served as the model for her book *Steamboat Gothic*. And the frilly house, with its elaborate galleries, does look like a steamboat run aground; it was built in 1856 by Edmond Bozonier Marmillion, and construction costs seem to have cleaned him out. (The original name of the house was San Frusquin, a French slang term meaning, roughly, "not a penny in my pocket.") Famed for its ornate ceiling frescoes and handsome millwork, the house is furnished according to inventories kept by the Marmillions.

Located on LA 44 in Reserve, San Francisco is open from 10:00 to 4:00. Phone 535-2341 for more information.

Oak Alley Plantation

The grounds of Oak Alley are among the most magnificent of any in the South. Twenty-eight huge, gnarled, moss-draped live oak trees—fourteen on each side of an alley from the road—were planted 250 years ago, long before the house was built in 1839. The Greek Revival mansion was originally named Bon Sejour, but riverboat passengers inevitably exclaimed over the oak alley and the name was eventually changed. The house and grounds have served as the set for several films, which will explain why it might look familiar. The exterior of the mansion is more impressive than the interior, which is furnished comfortably but not elegantly.

Overnight accommodations are in little screened-porch cottages on the grounds (rates start at $85) and a small restaurant serves breakfast and lunch. Located at 3645 LA 18 in Vacherie, the house has guided tours from 9:00 to 5:30 in March through October and from 9:00 to

5:00 in November through February. Phone 265-2487 (in Vacherie) or 523-4351 (direct line from New Orleans) for more information.

Tezcuco

The complex that is Tezcuco includes the main building, which dates from 1855; landscaped lawns with live oaks, gardens, and brick paths; and several outbuildings—chapel, blacksmith shop, commissary museum, and gazebos. The main house is a raised cottage made of cypress from the plantation's swamps and of bricks from its kiln. It is furnished with period pieces and features lovely cornices and ceiling medallions.

Tezcuco is located at 3138 LA 44 in Burnside. Its several B&B accommodations range from a third-story two-bedroom, two-bath suite in the main house ($150) to a small bedroom-and-bath cottage ($45). Docents in antebellum garb guide visitors daily from 9:00 to 5:00. Phone 562-3929 for more information.

The Cabin Restaurant

A mile north of Tezcuco, at the intersection of LA 22 and LA 44 in Burnside, the Cabin, housed in a 150-year-old slave cabin, is nothing if not casual. (If you hit it right at noon, you'll collide with several million tour-bus passengers.) Specialties are *étouffées*, po' boys, red beans and rice, and burgers, with prices hovering around $7 to $10. The Cabin's phone number is 473-3007.

Houmas House

One of the real knockout mansions, Houmas House, also in Burnside, is actually two houses connected by a carriageway. The older, rear house of four rooms dates from the late 1700s; the main, Greek Revival house was built in 1840. In 1858 John Burnside bought the house and twelve thousand acres for a million dollars—still a pretty good chunk of change. The wonderful old kitchen is cluttered with antique cooking utensils. The grounds are beautifully landscaped, and you can walk up on the levee to see the river.

Houmas House is on LA 942, Burnside. Costumed docents guide you through the house from 10:00 to 5:00 in February through October and from 10:00 to 4:00 in November through January. Call 473-7841 for more information.

Madewood Plantation

Another must-see mansion, Madewood is a glorious, twenty-one-room Greek Revival house bedecked with

---

ARCHITECTURAL GEMS

Architecture lovers should map out these sights for any plantation country touring.

- *Madewood Plantation (4250 LA 308, near Napoleonville)*
- *Nottoway Plantation (LA 1, near White Castle)*
- *Houmas House (LA 942 at Burnside)*
- *Rosedown Plantation (U. S. 61 at LA 10, St. Francisville)*
- *Milbank (102 Bank Street, Jackson)*

See Chapters 5, 6, 7, 8, and 11 for more gems.

white columns and double galleries. It was designed by famed Irish architect Henry Howard and built in 1846 for Colonel Thomas Pugh. Furnished with lovely antiques, it is also a bed-and-breakfast.

Madewood is at 4250 LA 308, Napoleonville. It's on the West Bank, and can be reached by crossing the Sunshine Bridge and following the "Bayou Plantation" sign to LA 70, Spur 70, and LA 308. Wine and cheeses and a Southern meal are included in the B&B rate ($165 in the main house or in Charlet House, a restored cottage on the grounds). Tours are conducted daily from 10:00 to 5:00. Call 369-7151 or 800/749-7151 for more information.

Lafitte's Landing Restaurant

On the West Bank, on the Sunshine Bridge access road near Donaldsonville, Lafitte's Landing is one of the state's finest restaurants. Chef John Folse, who can be seen working his culinary magic on PBS, is famous the world over for his innovative concoctions. His dishes are a blend of classic French and zesty Cajun tastes. Seafood is a specialty—trout Lafitte and pecan-smoked shrimp, for instance—but Folse doesn't limit himself, and the menu changes often. Dinner for two, without wine, costs about $60. Reservations are advised; call 473-1232. Lafitte's Landing is closed for dinner on Monday.

Nottoway Plantation

According to one story, when workers began construction on this monumental mansion they said there was "not a way" it could be built—hence the name. But built it was, and, as with Madewood, the architect was the irrepressible Henry Howard. An Italianate/Greek Revival extravaganza, the house has mind-boggling statistics: fifty-three thousand square feet of space, twenty-two columns, and two hundred windows, just for starters. The big white beauty is so luscious that one is tempted to take a slice and taste it. Of its sixty-four antique-filled rooms, the White Ballroom is a standout, with its original crystal chandeliers and white Corinthian columns. Thirteen of the rooms, in the main house and in outbuildings, are available for bed-and-breakfasting. You can swim in the pool, stroll around the considerable—and very lush— acreage, hike up on the levee to speak to the river, and have lunch or dinner (not included in the overnight rate) in the formal Randolph Hall restaurant.

Nottoway is on LA 1, near White Castle. Overnight rates are from $125 to $250. Touring is between 9:00 and 5:00. Phone 545-2730 or 346-8263 for more information.

Port Hudson

One of the pseudonyms of the Great River Road is U. S. 61, and if you follow it northward of Baton Rouge about fourteen miles you'll come to the Port Hudson State Commemorative Area. It seems somehow appropriate while touring antebellum plantations to stop and see a famous Civil War site. Within these 643 acres the longest siege in American military history took place. The siege began on May 23, 1863, with sixty-eight hundred Rebs pitted against thirty thousand Yankees. It lasted forty-eight days; the Rebels finally surrendered on July 9, 1863, after word reached them that Vicksburg had fallen. Just inside the park entrance is an interpretive center with exhibits and an observation tower. A boardwalk strings through the park and through the area where some of the fiercest fighting took place. There are also six miles of hiking trails, and sheltered picnic areas.

Audubon State Commemorative Area

Within this hundred-acre wooded site sits Oakley Plantation. In 1821 John James Audubon stayed here and tutored the young Eliza Pirrie, daughter of the plantation owner, while creating eighty of his famed Birds of America. The three-story house is designed in a West Indies style and furnished with Federal antiques. The walls are adorned with prints from Audubon's elephant folios.

About four miles north of Port Hudson, make a right turn on LA 965 to reach the Audubon State Commemorative Area. The grounds and house can be seen Wednesday through Sunday from 9:00 to 5:00. Phone 635-3739 for more information.

Rosedown Plantation House and Gardens

Three miles farther along lies the utterly charming St. Francisville, a town that has been described as two miles long and two yards wide. This is the home of Rosedown Plantation, a massive, two-story galleried structure that was built in 1835. Most of the museum-quality antiques are original to the house. The mansion is set in twenty-eight acres of luxuriantly landscaped gardens, where there are century-old camellias and azaleas and lovely marble statuary.

Rosedown is on U. S. 61 at LA 10. Tours are conducted March through October from 9:00 to 5:00 and November through February from 10:00 to 4:00. The phone number is 635-3332.

Catalpa Plantation

For a real treat, stop in and visit with Mrs. Mamie Thompson, whose lovely Victorian home is Catalpa. Mrs. Thompson is a descendant of the family that built and

---

NATURAL HIGHS

Those who enjoy seeing or learning about the great outdoors will want to catch these plantation country sights.

♦ *Grounds at Oak Alley (3645 LA 18, Vacherie)*
♦ *Grounds at Rosedown Plantation (U. S. 61 at LA 10, St. Francisville)*
♦ *Grounds at Audubon State Commemorative Area (LA 965, near St. Francisville)*

See Chapters 5, 6, 7, 8, and 11 for other natural highs.

---

lived in Rosedown well over 150 years ago. She has a stunning collection of silver, crystal, and china heirlooms as well as a delightful repertoire of stories.

Her house, three-and-a-half miles north of St. Francisville off U. S. 61, is set in a heavily wooded area at the end of an elliptical drive; it's a bit hard to find, but well worth the search. You can reach Mrs. Thompson at 635-3372, and you can visit her daily between 9:30 and 5:00 —except during December and January, when she receives visitors by appointment only.

Cottage Plantation

Cottage Plantation, built between 1795 and 1850, sits in four hundred wooded acres. The complex of original buildings includes a one-room schoolhouse, a teensy milk house, and a rustic old building that now houses Mattie's Restaurant, which is open only for dinner. The main house, which once hosted Andrew Jackson, is a long, low frame structure with chimneys and dormer windows. Bed-and-breakfast accommodations—five rooms, each with private bath—are in another original building a few steps from the main house.

Six miles north of St. Francisville—about two-and-a-half miles beyond Catalpa—the Cottage can be reached by turning off U. S. 61 highway onto Cottage Lane and ambling over a wooden bridge. B&B rates, which include a dip in the pool, begin at $90 (for a double). The house is open for touring daily from 9:00 to 5:00. Phone 635-3674 for more information.

Jackson

About fifteen miles northeast of St. Francisville lies the little town of Jackson, which has a most colorful past. Jackson is now in East Feliciana Parish, but in the early nineteenth century this was West Florida, a Spanish possession. This section was not included in the 1803 Louisiana Purchase, which miffed the English settlers; in 1810 seventy steaming Englishmen revolted against Spain and established the independent Republic of West Florida. The Republic was short lived; President Madison instructed Governor Claiborne to move in and annex the territory. At the Museum of the Republic of West Florida, on East College Drive in Jackson, exhibits depict the events of that period.

Jackson is on LA 10. The museum is open Tuesday through Saturday from 10:00 to 5:00 and Sunday from noon to 5:00. Admission is free (donations are happily accepted). Phone 634-7155 for more information.

Chapter Eleven
◆◆◆◆◆◆◆◆◆◆◆◆

Cajun Country

ACROSS the Mississippi from St. Francisville, you leave "English Louisiana" and step back into French Louisiana—not quite Cajun just yet. This section of French Louisiana was settled by Creoles in the 1700s.

First, know what you're looking for when setting out to explore Louisiana's famed French-American culture(s): This is not a miniature France, but it surely is not The South, although it is located geographically so. Standing between the doorways of an isolated past and the forces of the modern world, Louisiana's French heritage is remarkably well preserved. But its state of preservation is less interesting than its inherent qualities. You would have to search long and hard to find such an infectious vitality—the feeling that life and all its pleasures are to be enjoyed at all levels. Even the great wealth brought by the oil and gas industries in the Bayou State has failed to diminish the attitude here—that we all count, that we are all potential friends.

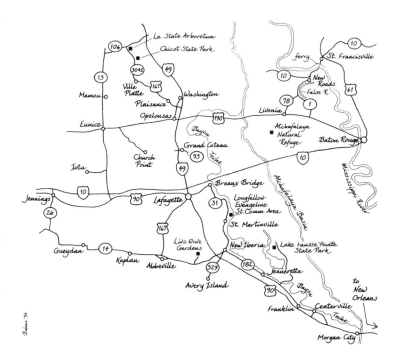

Cajun Country

"Allons!"

When you drive off the St. Francisville ferry, you'll be on LA 10 just outside of New Roads. The Pointe Coupée Bed and Breakfast (401 Richey Street, 504/638-6254 or 800/832-7412) in New Roads, operated by Al and Sidney Coffee, is in two historic houses—an 1835 creole cottage called the Samuel-Claiborne House and the turn-of-the-century Hebert House. Both have rooms with private baths and offer country breakfast in "Grandma's Kitchen." Rates begin at $55. With advance notice you can have a candlelight dinner in Hebert House; if you want to be up with the chickens to go fishing, you can have a sack lunch packed. Sidney has had her own tour company, and she can fill you in on all the things there are to do and see in this part of the state. The Coffees also operate the Coffee House Café (124 W. Main Street, 504/638-7859), a European-style café which specializes in updated versions of Old World creole recipes. The Coffee House Café sits on False River, an oxbow lake created when the Big Muddy changed course and left the lake behind. The lake is as blue as the river is red-muddy, and this is great fishing country. You'll see fishing cabins and boats tied up all along the lake.

On LA 1, the Pointe Coupée Parish Museum is six miles southwest of New Roads. Displays in the charming eighteenth-century building focus on the French connection between Canada and Louisiana. The museum is open Monday through Friday from 9:00 to 3:00, and Saturday from 10:00 to 3:00. Donations are appreciated.

Parlange Plantation, on False River (LA 1 near the intersection of LA 78), is a French colonial brick-and-

---

CAJUN LEXICON

- *Allons!*—Let's go!
- *Laissez les bons temps rouler*—Let the good times roll!
- *Fais-do-do* (pronounced fay doe doe)—a Cajun party, at which a lot of chank-a-chanking is done.
- *Chank-a-chank*—to dance to Cajun music
- *Lache pas la patate!*—Hang in there! (Literally, Don't let go of the potato.)

cypress home flanked by two-story *pigeonnières* (wings). Still a working plantation, the house was built in 1750 by relatives of the present owners, Mr. and Mrs. Walter Parlange, Jr., and it is a National Historic Landmark. It's open daily from 9:00 to 5:00, by appointment only. The phone number is 504/638-8410.

One of the state's best restaurants is Joe's Dreyfus Store on LA 77 in Livonia (504/637-2625). The casual restaurant, which specializes in Louisiana cuisine, is in a picturesque 1920s general store and pharmacy. It's open for lunch and dinner Tuesday through Saturday, and for lunch on Sunday.

Opelousas and Grand Coteau

U. S. 190 speeds right along westward from Creole country to Cajun Country, and leads into Opelousas, the state's third-oldest town. The folks at the Acadiana Tourist Information Center on U. S. 190 East, near I-49 (318/948-6263 or 800/424-5442) can give you plenty of free and friendly advice about things to do in the area. A small museum adjacent to the information center displays memorabilia pertaining to Jim Bowie, hero of the Texas revolution, who spent part of his childhood here.

Opelousas is a lovely little town with a very pretty historic district around the courthouse square. Renowned chef Paul Prudhomme was born here; you can see items pertaining to his early life in the Opelousas Museum and Interpretive Center (329 N. Main Street, 318/948-2589) —even the tiny washbasin in which Chef Paul was bathed as a baby. The museum boasts a lovely collection of antique clothing and a Civil War room. It is open Wednesday through Sunday from 9:00 to 5:00. Admission is free.

Just off courthouse square, the Doucas family at the Palace Café (167 W. Landry Street, 318/942-2142) has

been serving Cajun and Greek specialties since 1927. Be
sure to stop for Pete Doucas' specialty, fried chicken
salad, and some homemade baklava. On North Union
Street, the Holy Ghost Catholic Church, founded in 1920,
is the largest black Catholic parish in the United States.
Opelousas is also home to the International Cajun Joke-
Telling Contest, which is held each April (for information
call 318/948-4731). And don't forget that this is zydeco
country (a sizzling Black Creole version of Cajun music);
zydeco king Clifton Chenier was born near Opelousas in
Notlyville, on Bayou Teche just north of Lafayette. Every
year on the Saturday before Labor Day the Southwest
Louisiana Zydeco Music Festival takes off in Plaisance, a
stone's throw north of Opelousas on LA 10 and U. S.
167. Slim's Yi-Ki-Ki, probably the best zydeco dance hall
in the state (that is to say: in the nation), is outside
Opelousas (on U. S. 167, 318/942-9980).

A short drive south of Opelousas on I-49, LA 93
branches off to the east and leads into the peaceful little
town of Grand Coteau. Most of this tiny rural community is on the National Register of Historic Places. Grand
Coteau is a religious and educational community whose
most important structures are St. Charles Borromeo
Church and the Academy of the Sacred Heart. The present-day frame church, which replaced an 1820 structure,
was designed by New Orleans architect James Freret and
begun in 1879; it has an elaborate belfry with a rare
mansard roof, and a central spire of the Renaissance
revival style. The murals inside the church were painted
by Erasmus Humbrecht, who also painted the murals of
St. Louis Cathedral in New Orleans. (For information
about tours of the church, call 318/662-5279.)

Dating from 1821, the Academy of the Sacred Heart is
the oldest school in continuous existence in the worldwide
network of schools of the Society of the Sacred Heart.
Pilgrims come from all over the world to visit the Shrine

of St. John Berchmans—the only shrine in the United States erected on the exact place where a miracle occurred. In 1866 Berchmans, a Jesuit novice who had figured in the early history of the academy, appeared in a vision to a dying young woman. She was healed by the vision, and in 1888 Pope Leo XIII canonized John Berchmans. All of the documents and authentication pertaining to the Miracle of Grand Coteau are in the school's archives. The shrine is open for touring Sundays from 1:00 to 4:00 or by appointment; call 318/662-5275. Admission is $5. At the corner of King and Cherry Streets, the Kitchen Shop (318/662-3500) has a pretty patio where you can enjoy gourmet coffees, tea, and desserts. It's open Monday through Saturday from 9:00 to 5:00.

Not far from Grand Coteau, west of I-49 and just off LA 93, Chretien Point Plantation, built in 1831, is a stunning white-columned mansion that's open for touring and bed-and-breakfasting. In the 1930s an Opelousas photographer sent pictures of the house's stairway to Hollywood, and it eventually became the model for the stairs at Tara in *Gone with the Wind*. Ironically, long before Scarlett shot the Yankee from those stairs, a real shooting took place on the steps at Chretien Point. This house has a marvelous history as well as elegant furnishings and architecture. Tours are daily from 10:00 to 5:00 ($5 admission); five rooms (two with shared bath) are for overnighters (rates begin at $110). Phone 318/662-5876 for more information.

The little town of Washington, another charmer, lazes north of Opelousas on I-49. Washington is an old "steamboat town"; at the Museum and Tourist Center (402 N. Main Street, 318/826-3627), housed in old Washington Town Hall, you can watch a short video and see a collection of antique photos and artifacts from the steamboating era. This is also the place to make arrangements for tours of local historic homes. The museum is open Monday through Friday from 10:00 to 3:00, Saturday and Sunday from 9:00 to 4:00. And don't miss the Hinckley House (405 E. Dejean Street, 318/826-3906); this cypress house, built about 1800, is filled with steamboat memorabilia and antiques. It's open daily from 10:00 to 5:00, "by appointment or by chance." Admission is $3. De la Morandiere (515 S. John Street, 318/826-3510) is a house in the French West Indies style, with double verandahs; set on the banks of Bayou Courtableau, it is open daily from 10:00 to 5:00. Admission is $3. The Steamboat Warehouse (Main Street, 318/826-7227), which has a deck overlooking the bayou, is an unusual restaurant in a restored warehouse; this building, too, is a fine place for browsing through antiques and steamboating relics. Washington is home to Camellia Cove (205 W. Hill Street, 318/826-7362), a bed-and-breakfast in a house that dates from 1825. Three rooms with private bath are let to overnighters; rates start at $75.

Ville Platte and the Arboretum

Hitch up with LA 10 and go up to Ville Platte to visit Floyd's Record Store at 434 East Main Street (U. S. 167 southbound, 318/363-2184). This is a great fifties-style record store, crammed full of Cajun, zydeco, and swamp pop records, CDs, tapes, and videos. You can buy a Cajun accordion here, or a zydeco rub board—you can even buy accordion and rub-board earrings. The store is open Monday through Saturday from 8:00 to 5:00.

From Ville Platte, take LA 3042 eight miles north to see the Louisiana State Arboretum, adjacent to Chicot State Park. An interpretive shelter at the entrance has educational exhibits pertaining to the six-hundred-acre arboretum. A natural for naturalists, the arboretum is laced with nature trails, creeks, and footbridges and

NATURAL HIGHS

Those who enjoy seeing or learning about the great outdoors will want to catch these Cajun Country sights.

- *Louisiana State Aboretum (LA 3042, north of Ville Platte)*
- *Cajun Prairie Preservation Project (corner of M. L. K. Drive and Magnolia Street, Eunice)*—preserves and protects the prairie wildflowers.
- *Lafayette Natural History Museum and Planetarium (637 Girard Park Drive, Lafayette)*
- *Live Oak Gardens (284 Rip van Winkle Road, off LA 14 southwest of New Iberia)*
- *Avery Island Jungle Gardens (LA 329, south of New Iberia)*
- *Atchafalaya Basin (east of Lafayette at Henderson)*—an eerily beautiful eight-hundred-thousand-acre swamplands.
- *The Creole Nature Trail (LA 27)*
- *Lake Fausse Pointe State Park (near Loreauville)*—has overnight cabins and boat rentals.

See Chapters 5, 6, 7, 8, and 10 for more natural highs.

graced with a variety of labeled trees and plants indigenous to Louisiana. One of the prettiest places in the state,
it's open every day from dawn to dusk, and there's no
charge for taking in its considerable charms.

Prairie Cajun Country

From the Arboretum, pick up LA 106 and head west to
LA 13 and then south to Mamou. There's not a thing in
the world in Mamou except Fred's Lounge (420 S. Sixth
Street, 318/468-5411)—but you might want to plan your
trip so as to be at Fred's any Saturday morning between
8:00 and noon. Fred Tate's place is a bar, notwithstanding the name; it isn't a cocktail lounge or anything fancy
like that. But for more than forty years live Cajun radio
shows, replete with band, have been broadcast from Fred's
every Saturday morning. The center of the small room is
roped off to protect the band and the storytellers and the
equipment from the couples waltzing and chank-a-chanking around the ropes (*chank-a-chank* is Cajun for dancing). One big handwritten sign implores people not to
stand on the cigarette machine or jukebox; another ad-
vises folks that this is a bar and not a dance hall and if
they're injured while dancing it isn't the fault of the
management.

   At least part of the reason for the signs in Fred's has to
do with the wild Courir de Mardi Gras, or Mardi Gras
run. Little villages such as Mamou, Church Point, Eunice,
and Iota are in the flat Cajun prairie country—very
different from the bayou country of their cousins farther
east. On Mardi Gras—the day before Ash Wednesday—
masked and costumed horseback riders thunder over the
prairies, stopping at farmlands and picking up food and
folks for a big celebration in the town square. This is by
no means a tourist event; in fact, you can't really see the
goings on out in the country. The riders, as the saying

goes, have their own agenda, and it has to do with an age-old tradition. This is a family-oriented affair; throughout the day downtown events feature live Cajun and zydeco music, food and souvenir vendors, children's costume contests, and the like. For more information about the Courir de Mardi Gras, call 318/457-2565.

Continue south on LA 13 to Eunice—a very happening place indeed. Eunice is home to the Rendez-Vous des Cajuns, a live radio show that broadcasts every Saturday night from 6:00 to 8:00 at the Liberty Theater (corner of S. Second Street and Park Avenue, 318/457-7389). A restored 1924 movie house, the theater was included in the Smithsonian's Great American Movie Theaters Preservation Press Guide. This show is an absolute must-see. A blend of the Grand Ole Opry, "Louisiana Hayride," and "Prairie Home Companion," the show is done mostly in French—but you do not have to know the language to enjoy it. In addition to the joke-telling and the repartee, there's plenty of dancing; the first several rows of the theater have been removed to make room for all the two-stepping that goes on here. Get there early: They sometimes have to lock the doors at 5:30 because the place is already packed. Admission is $2. Just behind the theater, the Prairie Acadian Cultural Center (corner of S. Third Street and Park Avenue, 318/457-8499) traces the history of the "prairie Cajuns" in several well-mounted displays and presents demonstrations and special exhibits. It's open daily from 9:00 to 6:00. Admission is free.

The Eunice Museum (220 S. C. C. Duson Drive, 318/457-6540) is on the site of the town's birthplace. It was here, in 1893–94, that C. C. Duson sold the first land sites and named the town for his wife. The museum, in an old railroad depot, has collections of Cajun music, antique toys, and railroad memorabilia; exhibits trace the history of Cajun Mardi Gras, and the museum has souvenirs and Cajun crafts. Hours are Tuesday through

---

CULTURE

Cajun Country has something to offer to those with a cultural bent.

- *Zigler Museum (411 Clara Street, Jennings)*
- *University Art Museum (University of Southwestern Louisiana, Lafayette)*
- *Lafayette Museum (1122 Lafayette Street, Lafayette)*

See Chapters 4, 5, and 8 for other cultural treats.

Saturday from 8:00 to noon and 1:00 to 5:00. Admission is free. At the corner of M. L. K. Drive and Magnolia Street, the Cajun Prairie Preservation Project (318/457-4497), another good place for nature lovers, sees to the restoration and preservation of the wildflowers and plants of the prairie. You can overnight at the Seale Guesthouse (on LA 13, 318/457-3753), where accommodations range from a two-bedroom cottage to suites with shared baths to rooms with private baths. Rates start at $55. And you can get a good taste of this part of the state at Nick's (123 Second Street, 318/457-4921).

Continuing south on LA 13, you'll come to Interstate 10. Before heading east to Lafayette, drive a bit less than twenty miles west on the interstate to see the little town of Jennings. Jennings has a lovely restored Main Street; the town's pride and joy is the restored W. H. Tupper General Merchandise Museum (311 N. Main, 318/821-5532). The store opened in 1910, and when it closed in 1949 everything in it was frozen in time. With its antique clothes and games, sewing machines and yard goods, and old-time auto parts, scales, and meat-wrapping paper, it's a time capsule of life in the early twentieth century. The museum can be visited Monday through Saturday from 10:00 to 6:00. Admission is $2.

In contrast to the old-fashioned country store, the Zigler Museum (411 Clara Street, 318/824-0114) is a modern museum whose several rooms include displays of European and American artists, a collection of Louisiana wildlife dioramas, and rotating exhibits displayed in the central galleries. The collection is housed in the stately family home of the late Mr. and Mrs. Fred B. Zigler. Hours are Tuesday through Saturday from 9:00 to 5:00 and Sunday from 1:00 to 5:00. Admission is $3. For good down-home eats, go to Donn E.'s (318/824-3402) on LA 26, a half mile north of I-10; it's open daily for lunch and dinner, and it couldn't be more casual. And for a wonderful place to lay your head, try Creole Rose Manor (214

ARCHITECTURAL GEMS

Architecture lovers should map out these sights for any Cajun Country touring.

♦ *Shadows-on-the-Teche (317 E. Main Street, New Iberia)*
♦ *Chretien Point (off I-49 and LA 93, near Sunset)*
♦ *À la Bonne Veillée (LA 339, southwest of Lafayette)*—a restored nineteenth century Acadian cottage and B&B.
♦ *The antebellum mansions of Franklin*

See Chapters 5, 6, 7, 8, and 10 for more gems.

W. Plaquemine Street, 318/824-3145 or 824-4936), a bed-and-breakfast with family heirlooms and friendly hosts.

From Jennings, drop down south on LA 26 to Lake Arthur and turn east on LA 14, which goes through Gueydan and Kaplan to the little town of Abbeville. This is a pretty sleepy little burg—until you get to Cajun Downs, that is. Called a "bush track" because it's out in the bush, Cajun Downs (318/893-8160 or 318/893-0421) has been racing critters of all sorts for more than a hundred years. The track is a slash of red dirt cut through a canefield, and there's nothing fancy like bleachers. But the races here are wild and woolly—six or eight of them on Sundays—and the place is as casual and as colorful as you can get. The track is on LA 338 off the LA 14 bypass in Abbeville. And before leaving Abbeville, stop in for boiled crawfish at Richard's Seafood Patio (1516 S. Henry Street, 318/893-1693); it's open daily for dinner December through June.

The Capital of French Louisiana

From Abbeville, head north on U. S. 167 to Lafayette, which bills itself as the Capital of French Louisiana. A major metropolis compared to the little villages of Abbeville and Mamou, Lafayette is a good place to establish a base if you plan to stay a spell in Cajun Country; it has much to offer in its own right, and you can make easy day trips in all directions. Stop in at the Lafayette Convention and Visitors Commission (Evangeline Thruway at Willow, 318/232-3808 or 800/346-1958) and load up the tote bags with maps and brochures on Acadiana.

Two of Lafayette's attractions in particular trace the history of the Cajuns. One is a re-creation of an early Cajun/Creole settlement; the other is the Acadian Cultural Center, a unit of the Jean Lafitte National Park. The

Acadian Village is a depiction of a small bayou settlement; several authentic nineteenth-century structures—including a pretty white chapel, a blacksmith shop, a general store, and houses—were moved to this site from their original locations, and they now contain exhibits that characterize early life in the region. During December the village draws thousands to see its wonderland of Christmas lights. Acadian Village is located south of town on LA 342 off Ridge Road, ten miles south of I-10. It is open daily from 10:00 to 5:00. Admission is $5.

The Jean Lafitte National Historical Park maintains units in New Orleans, Barataria, Thibodeaux, Eunice, and Lafayette. Each pertains to the culture of South Louisiana; as with the Eunice unit, the Lafayette center focuses on the Acadians. The Acadian Cultural Center is a spacious building with several rooms in which audio/visual exhibits are devoted to various aspects of Cajun life. You can watch a video on Acadiana, and buy books pertaining to the region. It's at 501 Fisher Road, and is open daily from 8:00 to 5:00. Admission is free. Call 318/232-0789 for more information. The Lafayette Natural History Museum and Planetarium (116 Polk Street, 318/268-5544), open every day, is in a lovely park setting and has changing exhibits that pertain to the natural environment of the region.

This being Cajun Country, where the motto is *Laissez les bons temps rouler* ("Let the good times roll"), naturally there are festivals galore in Lafayette. Folks in these parts really let their hair down during Cajun Mardi Gras, an eye-popping extravaganza of costumes and parades. Another big event is Festival International de Louisiane (P.O. Box 4008, Lafayette, LA 70502; 318/232-8086), held annually in April. Past festivals have drawn four hundred dancers, musicians, and artisans from Africa, Canada, the Caribbean, Europe, and the Americas. The festive September blowout is Festival Acadiens, which focuses on the food and music of Acadiana. For more information contact the Lafayette Convention and Visitors Commission, P.O. Box 52066, Lafayette, LA 70502, or phone 318/232-3808, 800/346-1958 (U.S.), or 800/543-5340 (Canada).

Since food is celebrated in these parts as much as music, you won't have a bit of trouble finding eatables. Café Vermilionville (not to be confused with the theme park) is an upscale restaurant in a lovely eighteenth-century inn on the banks of Bayou Vermilion (1304 W. Pinhook Road, 318/237-0100). Both Prejean's (3480 U. S. 167 North, 318/896-3247) and Randol's (2320 Kaliste Saloom Road, 318/981-7080) serve up Cajun food and live Cajun dancing music nightly. The same is true for Belizaire's over in Crowley (2307 N. Patterson Avenue, 318/788-2501), a fit place both to eat and to beat your feet. Cajun dance halls, incidentally, are family-oriented places, and there are more around here than you can shake a stick at. Out on the dance floors you'll see grizzled granddads waltzing and two-stepping with their little toddling grandkids and young couples twirling and whirling to beat the band. Cajun dancing is great good fun, and it doesn't matter if you are overly endowed with left feet—the music will lure you to the floor, and you'll be surprised at the friendly folk who'll be happy to show you how dancing's done, Cajun-style.

Lafayette is loaded up with hotels and chain motels; there's a Hilton Hotel (1521 W. Pinhook Road, 318/235-6111 or 800/332-2586) and the Hotel Acadiana (1801 W. Pinhook Road, 318/233-8120 or 800/531-5900). There are some wonderful bed-and-breakfasts in and around Lafayette, too. Bois des Chenes (338 N. Sterling, 318/233-7816) offers three guest rooms, all with private baths, in an 1890s carriage house in the center of town; doubles start at $95. À la Bonne Veillée (LA 339, about fifteen minutes southwest of Lafayette; 318/937-5495) is a restored, early-nineteenth-century two-bedroom Acadian cottage, with Acadian antiques, two fireplaces, rocking chairs on the front porch, phones, TVs, and complete privacy. Because of the intimacy of the cottage, it's rented only to a family or to two couples traveling together; cost is $100 for one couple.

Just north of Lafayette, Prudhomme's Cajun Café (4676 N. E. Evangeline Thruway, 318/896-7964), the restaurant of Enola Prudhomme—estimable sister of the estimable Chef Paul—turns out marvelous Cajun fare. The most expensive item on the menu is around $15. Take exit 7 off I-49.

Crawfish and Catalans

A ten-minute drive east of Lafayette on LA 94 will take you to Breaux Bridge, which bills itself as the Crawfish Capital of the World; the annual Crawfish Festival each May draws more than one hundred thousand to this little village. Between festivals, though, Breaux Bridge boasts Mulate's, a Cajun café and dance hall of considerable fame. Live music and great, inexpensive seafood put it on the map. A roadhouse at 325 Mills Avenue, it's open every day for breakfast, lunch, and dinner and offers live music accompanying lunch and dinner. Phone 318/332-4648 for more information.

From Breaux Bridge, LA 31 is a pretty country drive that strings alongside Bayou Teche, the state's longest bayou. On the outskirts of St. Martinville you'll come to the Longfellow-Evangeline State Commemorative Area, a beautiful 157-acre park with picnic grounds, an interpretive center, several nineteenth-century cypress cottages, and a boat launch.

St. Martinville itself was both a major debarkation point for the Acadians expelled from their homes in present-day Nova Scotia and a refuge for French royalists somewhat eager to escape the guillotine during the French Revolution. Not a lot happens now in St. Martinville, but in its eighteenth-century heyday it was known as "Petit Paris" and was a center for royal balls and opera. The exhibits at the Petit Paris Museum on the church square (131 S. Main Street, 318/394-7334) pertain to the little town's rich history as well as to Cajun Mardi Gras. Admission is one dollar. The Church of St. Martin de Tours, adjacent to the museum, is the mother church of the Acadians. The parish dates from 1765, and the present-day church was built in 1837 (103 S. Main, 318/394-3455). Stroll around behind the church to see the ancient cemetery and the statue of Evangeline; thirties film star Dolores del Rio posed for the bronze statue, which was donated to the town after *The Romance of Evangeline* was filmed here in 1929. This is "Evangeline" country; Longfellow's poem of that name was based on the torturous exodus of the Acadians from their Nova Scotia homeland. The Evangeline and Gabriel of the famous poem were, in real life, Emmeline Labiche and Louis Arceneaux. The real-life lovers are said to have met for the last time beneath the branches of one of St. Martinville's most famous attractions—the spreading Evangeline Oak, which sits on the banks of bottle-green Bayou Teche. The Old Castillo Hotel, some of whose rooms overlook the oak and the bayou, has served variously as an inn, a girls' school, and a hall for glamorous royalist balls; nowadays it's a bed-and-breakfast with five rooms to let, a fine restaurant, and Acadian hosts who enjoy helping visitors "pass a good time."

Continuing southeasterly on LA 31, stop at New Iberia—originally settled by Spaniards from the Iberian coast—to see the splendid Shadows-on-the-Teche historic house (317 E. Main, 318/369-6446); built by sugar planter David Weeks, it dates from 1834. This big brick house, a property of the National Trust for Historic

HISTORICAL HIGHLIGHTS

History buffs might like to try this Cajun Country tour.

♦ *Acadian Cultural Center (501 Fisher Road, Lafayette)*—a museum of the early Creole/Cajun cultures.

♦ *Acadian Village (LA 342 off Ridge Road, Lafayette)*—a re-creation of an early Acadian village.

♦ *Tupper Museum (311 N. Main Street, Jennings)*—a preserved early-twentieth-century general store.

♦ *Prairie Acadian Cultural Center (S. Third Street and Park Avenue, Eunice)*—traces the history of the "prairie Cajuns."

♦ *Opelousas Museum and Interpretive Center (329 N. Main Street, Opelousas)*

♦ *St. Martinville (LA 31, near Lafayette)*— the site of Longfellow's poem "Evangeline."

See Chapter 4 for more history stops.

Preservation, is not to be missed. Although it's on the main street, you have to look for it; it's almost hidden by scrims of Spanish moss dripping from old live oaks. It's open daily from 9:00 to 4:30. Admission is $6. New Iberia's other big splash is the nation's oldest rice mill: The Conrad Rice Mill (309 Ann Street, 318/367-6163) can be toured between 9:00 and 5:00 Monday through Saturday, for $3. Its companion, the Konriko Company

Store, presents a slide show on Cajun culture and sells local food and craft items. If your mouth is fixed for food, Lagniappe Too (204 E. Main, 318/365-9419) is a good choice. Open every day but Sunday, it's a casual place for quiches and sandwiches, and it has a fabulous collection of handmade dolls lining the walls.

New Iberia is the jumping-off place for visiting Live Oak Gardens and Avery Island. Live Oak Gardens, also called Jefferson Island, was the winter home of nine-teenth-century actor Joseph Jefferson, who toured the country portraying Rip van Winkle. His 1870 home is a three-story Gothic-*cum*-Moorish house with lovely fur-nishings, a belvedere, and a verandah for enjoying the views. The twenty acres of gardens were reconstructed following a disaster. Although drilling for oil in and around Lake Peigneur, adjacent to the Jefferson home, had been going on for years, in 1980 drills pierced the walls of the vast salt mine beneath the property. The walls caved in and the lake flooded the mine, its waters sucking down huge barges, boats, and most of the oil rig, all of which washed into the mine like unplugged water from a bathtub. Miraculously, no one was killed. Live Oak Gar-dens reopened in 1984 after extensive repairs; now, in addition to tours of the house and gardens, you can take a forty-five-minute boat tour on Lake Peigneur. There's also a pleasant café overlooking the lake.

Live Oak Gardens is southwest of New Iberia, off LA 14, at 284 Rip van Winkle Road. The $8.50 admission includes the boat ride. Phone 318/365-3332 for more information.

It may not be universally known that the Tabasco sauce that flavors many a Bloody Mary was created in South Louisiana, and continues to be produced by descendants of Edmund McIlhenny, who first concocted the hot-hot sauce in the 1800s. The factory can be toured on Avery Island—another salt dome rather than an island in the traditional sense. Avery Island is also known for its two-hundred-acre Jungle Gardens, a splendid place where flowers and plants bloom year round and hundreds of birds wing in to sit a spell in the Bird City sanctuary. Avery Island is seven miles south of New Iberia, on LA 329. It is open Monday through Friday from 9:00 to 4:00 and Saturday from 9:00 to noon. Tours of the factory are free. The Jungle Gardens are open daily from 9:00 to 5:00. Admission is $5. Phone 318/369-6243 or 365-8173 for more information.

A favorite eating place in this area is the Yellow Bowl (318/276-5512), about ten miles below New Iberia and three miles east of Jeanerette on LA 182. The casual restaurant has been serving Cajun things like crawfish *étouffée* since 1927. It's only open Thursday and Friday for both lunch and dinner; on Saturday it serves dinner only and on Sunday lunch only. If you can make it during one of those times, you're in for a fine and inexpensive feast.

Continuing southward on LA 182, you'll arrive in Franklin, another very pretty Teche town. From the downtown Park on the Teche there's a knockout view of the lazy bayou. Franklin, although in the heart of Cajun Country, was founded by the English. The town is noted for its plethora of elegant antebellum mansions, most of them Greek Revival houses filled with nineteenth-century Louisiana antiques. Admission to each is around $5 or $6. Some are standouts. Oaklawn Manor, dating from around 1837, sits in a grove of live oak trees. Open daily from 10:00 to 4:00, it's on Irish Bend Road, off LA 182. The phone number is 318/828-0434. The Grevemberg House Museum, at City Park, was built about 1850. It is open Thursday through Sunday from 10:00 to 4:00. Arlington Plantation, a private residence overlooking Bayou Teche a mile east of town on LA 182, is open by appointment only; call 318/828-2644.

Keeping on a southeasterly swoop, you'll merge with U. S. 90 after you go through Centerville, and U. S. 90 is where you'll stay until you move on up to little old New Orleans (unless you've gotten attached to Louisiana's meandering country roads and aim to veer off in search of some other adventure).

Offshore of Morgan City, on November 14, 1947, the Kerr-McGee rig no. 16 struck oil and ushered in the "black gold rush" that brought prosperity to the state. The oil boom fizzled in the 1980s, and Louisiana's Gulf Coast has been in dire straits ever since. To add to these troubles, Morgan City and other towns along the coast were battered by Hurricane Andrew in 1992. The possibility exists that the worst is yet to come: Morgan City sits smack on the Atchafalaya River, and the Atchafalaya Bay gapes just a few miles to the south. For a long time now Old Man River has been licking at the levees in an effort to get at the Atchafalaya. So far, at least, the U. S. Army Corps of Engineers has managed to keep the river in check.

PART THREE
••••••••••••••
THE BEST PLACES

Chapter Twelve
◆◆◆◆◆◆◆◆◆◆◆◆◆

Hotels, Guesthouses, and B&Bs

A BOUT THE ONLY kinds of accommodations you won't find in the Crescent City are seaside resorts on white sand beaches and Alpine cabins clutching the banks of gurgling mountain streams. That's because there are neither beaches nor mountains in these flat swamplands.

New Orleans is best known for the French Quarter's guesthouses tucked away in quaint nineteenth-century creole town houses and cottages, and for the Garden District's bed-and-breakfasts in handsome mansions. Many are small, family run, and very European in style and ambience. All are air-conditioned—as is everything in New Orleans except Lafitte's Blacksmith Shop, horse-drawn carriages, and bicycles—and most have pools but no restaurants, lounges, or bars. They do offer personal attention, and many have repeat visitors for whom the guesthouse is a second home and the proprietors an extended family.

New Orleans has been ranked the nation's second most popular convention city, and a plethora of splashy, high-tech, high-rise hotels cater to conventioneers. Most of these hotels are in the Central Business District, or CBD: major chains awash with restaurants, bars, lounges, pools, fitness centers, and everything else you can also find in Cleveland, Des Moines, or Dallas. However, since the French Quarter is the city's main draw, the big hotels do make attempts at duplicating the Quarter's unique flavor. And the few large hotels in the Quarter do combine an Old World ambience with all the comforts modern technology can provide.

In between the guesthouses and the high-tech hotels are some small hotels that provide the personal attention of the former and the amenities of the latter. Chain motels abound, downtown as well as in outlying areas, including the airport. Save them for turnpike and expressway travel.

Rates are accurate at press time, but there is a caveat writ large regarding hotel prices. New Orleans has no clearly defined high and low seasons. During certain major annual events—namely Mardi Gras, Jazz Fest, and the Sugar Bowl—rates go through the ceiling and may reach at least double those quoted here. For those events, most hotels have a three- to five-day minimum stay; some require full payment in advance. Rates also zoom skyward during big conventions—say, when fifty thousand Shriners turn up in town—or on a busy Fourth of July weekend. Be wise and nail down a hotel's cancellation and refund policy when you make a reservation. In general, rates are rock bottom during the summer, when you can usually buy an attractive hotel package. During Creole Christmas—the whole month of December—most hotels offer special moderate "Papa Noël" rates.

The hotel tax is a dizzying 11 percent (5 percent in B&Bs with fewer than ten rooms); tacked onto that is a city tax that ranges from one dollar to $3 per room per night, depending upon the number of rooms. The "extra person" charge is around $15 or $20. In many places, children under twelve or so can stay free in the same room with their parents.

Zip codes vary throughout the city; the French Quarter alone has three separate zips.

The Very Best

WINDSOR COURT. No point in beating around the bush: The city's only five-star hotel is also the city's best, period. It richly deserves all the accolades it continues to collect.

The brainchild of James Coleman, avid Anglophile and honorary British consul, the hotel opened in 1984, boasting a $6 million collection of seventeenth-, eighteenth-, and nineteenth-century English art. Princess Margaret and her son, the Viscount Linley; Prince and Princess Michael of Kent; and Princess Alexandra are among the royals who have hung out in the hotel; and this was also Kevin Costner's hideaway during the filming of *JFK*. But don't expect a snooty staff and off-putting ambience: The staff is not only impeccably trained, but friendly as well. They also get a kick out of tackling challenging tasks. For a wedding reception for a couple who were both medical professionals, the bride and groom arrived at the hotel on stretchers. The wedding party swept through the luxurious lobby, passed out sunglasses to some rather startled hotel guests, and then adjourned to the ballroom, where they donned shades and boogied with the Blues Brothers.

The digs here are decidedly plush. There are 264 suites and fifty-eight rooms, with four-posters, canopied beds, rich fabrics, framed artworks, and oversized marble baths with such niceties as magnifying mirrors. Business travelers find well-lighted desks and business services. The phones do everything except rub your back—but there's an in-house masseuse for that.

Other creature comforts are the outdoor Olympic-sized pool (surrounded by umbrella tables) and a health club, sauna, and Jacuzzi. The top-notch Grill Room serves breakfast, lunch, and dinner. And every afternoon, movers and shakers and simple folk alike gather for afternoon tea, scones, and chamber music in the cushy lobby lounge, Le Salon, where lunch is also served.

Rates are per room or suite rather than per person. Guest rooms run from $200 to $250; junior suites, $275 to $325; full suites, $300 to $450; and two-bedroom suites, $575 to $750. 300 Gravier Street, New Orleans 70130, 504/523-6000, 800/262-2662, fax 504/596-4513. AE, DC, MC, V.

Guesthouses and B&Bs

FRENCH QUARTER MAISONETTES. With rates ranging from $50 to $74, this is the kind of place budget travelers dream about. Located in the residential section of the Quarter (directly across the street from the posh Soniat House), it is a short walk from the French Market and Jackson Square. A half block away is Croissant d'Or, whose fresh-baked croissants and gourmet coffees lure legions of Quarterites each morning for breakfast.

The entrance is through a broad cast-iron gate and a carriageway, beyond which is a lovely courtyard with a fountain. The reception area is on the second floor of an 1825 town house that's home to the *chatelaine*, Mrs. Junius Underwood, an Old Worldly, French Quarter legend. Now in ill health, Mrs. Underwood has put day-to-day operations in the capable hands of Bud, who holds down the registration desk, and Jesse, the porter who has been at the Maisonettes for almost forty years. Each of the seven simply furnished apartments opens onto the courtyard, and each has a small TV and microwave (but no phone). Although there are few frills, there is a wealth of personal attention and helpful advice. Small, well-behaved pets are accepted, but children under twelve are not.

1130 Chartres Street, New Orleans 70116, 504/524-9918. No credit cards. Closed in July.

JOSEPHINE GUEST HOUSE. On the fringe of the Garden District, at the corner of Josephine and Prytania Streets, a big white Italianate mansion dating from 1870 is the home of Dan Fuselier and his wife, Mary Ann Weilbaecher. Happily, it's also a bed-and-breakfast in which guests can enjoy the couple's vast collection of antiques and reproductions. One of the most dramatic pieces is a huge ebony bed from Germany, inlaid with ivory and bone. An eighteenth-century banquet table, a Gothic refectory table, and Dutch marquetry daybeds are also impressive. Dan and Mary Ann keep up to speed on what's doing in the Big Easy, and they like to give their guests pointers on the best things to see and do. The St. Charles Streetcar is one block away.

All six rooms have a private bath. A breakfast of homemade breads, juices, and rich *café au lait* is served on Wedgwood china with fine cutlery. Rates are from $75 to $135. 1450 Josephine Street, New Orleans 70130, 504/524-6361. AE, MC, V.

LAFITTE'S GUEST HOUSE. On a quiet corner, but only four blocks from Bourbon Street activity, Lafitte's was built in 1849 as a manor house for P. J. Gelieses. The present-day owner has furnished it with his private collection of antiques and reproductions. The parlor is a marvel of Victoriana, with red velvet swag drapes and matching chairs, an Oriental rug, a satin-upholstered settee, and a handsome carved mantelpiece. Complimentary wine and cheeses are served in the parlor during the cocktail hour.

Most of the rooms feature canopy or half tester beds, marble-topped tables, and crystal chandeliers. About half of them have a full bath; the others have only showers. The only contemporary room is Room 5, which occupies the former carriagehouse off the courtyard and has a loft bedroom overlooking the downstairs sitting room; the oversized shower was converted from a coal bin. Room 40, which extends over the entire upper floor, houses a blend of antiques and wicker, and provides a great view of the Quarter; it is also one of two rooms with a wet bar, and its two queen-size beds and sleeper sofa make it roomy enough to accommodate six. The double balconies at the rear are enclosed in white latticework, providing privacy during your complimentary breakfast of juice, tea or coffee, and croissants.

The Lafitte does not have a pool or a restaurant, but it is in close proximity to one of the city's favorite and most famous watering holes, Lafitte's Blacksmith Shop, just across the street.

Weekday room rates begin at $85. Suites soar to $280. 1003 Bourbon Street, New Orleans 70116. 504/581-2678, 800/331-7971. AE, MC, V.

LAMOTHE HOUSE. In 1833, Miss Marie Virginie Lamothe sold her property on Esplanade Avenue to her brother, Jean Lamothe, a wealthy sugar planter who came to New Orleans from the West Indies. The mansion he built for his family in 1839 was one of the city's first double town houses, divided by a carriageway that swept from the street to the rear courtyard. Later owners made considerable renovations to the house. The carriageway was enclosed to create the main entrance hall; other alterations, made in 1860, include the handcarved Corinthian columns that frame the front doors; the twin winding stairways that lead to the second floor reception area and the two third-floor suites; and the elaborate millwork, cornices, and ceiling medallions.

A gilt-and-etched-glass chandelier hangs in the reception area, where walls are adorned with lovely oil paintings. In the adjacent formal dining room, where complimentary coffee and pastries are served each morning, an elaborate carved mantel protects an original fireplace. Carved half tester beds, four-posters, and Victorian furnishings dressed in velvets and brocades decorate the nine rooms and eleven suites. The suites in the main house are large but rather dark, and baths are quite small. Room 102, the Mallard Suite, has elaborate furnishings hand-carved by Prudent Mallard, a well-known nineteenth-century New Orleans cabinetmaker. Room 117, across a courtyard paved with original flagstones that traveled the Atlantic as ship's ballast, has a large, light-filled sitting room and bedroom separated by a floor-to-ceiling brick fireplace and a spacious bath.

Lamothe House has neither a pool nor a restaurant. Parking is free. Rooms are $87 to $97, and suites are $135 to $175. 621 Esplanade Avenue, New Orleans 70116. 504/947-1161, 800/367-5858, fax 504/943-6536. AE, MC, V.

MELROSE MANSION. In the 1880s, plantation owner George Lanaux and his family lived and entertained lavishly in a classic Gothic/Victorian mansion, replete with gingerbread trim, white-columned galleries, dormers, turret, and tower. In that bygone era, their elaborate home was but one of the fine mansions that lined broad, tree-shaded Esplanade Avenue on the fringe of the French Quarter. The Lanaux family occupied the house for some thirty years, after which the mansion changed hands a number of times. In 1976, Melvin Jones and his partner, Sidney Torres, bought the house from Bourbon Street entertainer Chris Owens, who had lived there with her husband, the late Sol Owens. In 1988 Jones and Torres began an eighteen-month, $1.5 million restoration. When the bed-and-breakfast opened in January 1990, the first person to sign the guest register was Lady Bird Johnson.

Melrose Mansion—the Mel is Melvin Jones; the Rose his wife, Rosemary—has leaded glass windows, wood floors polished to a high sheen, period furnishings upholstered in velvet and brocade, and ceilings that soar into the stratosphere. Its four rooms and four suites, decorated with a mix of twentieth-century amenities (wet bars and whirlpool baths) and nineteenth-century charm, are filled with antiques; the Prince Edward Suite has a queen-size sleigh bed. The real knockout is the Donecio Suite, which has in its turret a marble whirlpool (and a frosted ice bucket of champagne within easy reach) as well as a private verandah that overlooks Esplanade Avenue and the French Quarter. A decanter of Courvoisier is in each room, as are down pillows, fine milled soaps, coffeemakers, and fresh flowers. Other *luxe* touches include a heated pool, evening cocktails, and complimentary airport limo. The Sol Owens Suite is the fitness center, with its adjacent sitting room a fit place for relaxing and reading.

Rates are from $250 to $475. 937 Esplanade Avenue, New Orleans 70116, 504/944-2255. Personal checks accepted. AE, MC, V.

OLIVIER HOUSE. During the 1830s, when New Orleans' Golden Age was beginning to glow, one of the outstanding architects working in the French Quarter was J. N. B. DePouilly, who arrived in the city after graduating from the École des Beaux Arts in Paris. In 1836 he designed a town house for Marianne Bienvenue Olivier, the widow of a well-heeled Creole plantation owner. Mme. Olivier needed a house in town large enough to accommodate her fifty children and grandchildren. The building had become a rundown apartment house when Jim and Kathryn Danner bought, renovated, and transformed it into a guesthouse in 1970.

The Olivier House is in a class by itself: People either love it or hate it. Wildly popular with legions of repeat guests who are captivated by its casual, informal atmosphere, it is equally maddening to anyone who is turned off by that carefree ambience. Europeans adore it, in part because it reminds them of the informal inns back home. The hotel is also popular with artists, actors, and writers. Maestro Anton Coppola stayed here when he was in town to conduct the opera orchestra, until his nephew, film director Francis Ford Coppola, bought a house in the Quarter.

Each of the forty-two rooms and suites varies in size and decor. Some have period antiques and reproductions; others have contemporary or traditional furnishings; many have kitchenettes with microwaves. A few of the rooms are small and dark, but there are large, airy rooms and suites as well. Room 112, for example, is a huge, sunny two-story suite replete with skylight. Rooms 107 and 103 have French doors leading directly out to the pool area, which is banked with tropical greenery. A charmer is Room 114, a little cottage tucked away behind its own peaceful, private courtyard near the pool.

Rooms begin at $95 for a double. Suites run from $175 to $210. 828 Toulouse Street, New Orleans 70112, 504/525-8456, fax 504/529-2006. AE, CB, DC, MC, V.

SONIAT HOUSE. On a quiet residential street in the lower French Quarter, the exclusive twenty-four-room Soniat House, which sits on land that once belonged to the nearby Old Ursuline Convent, occupies two early-nineteenth-century town houses. In 1829, Joseph Soniat du Fossat, the son of a military engineer who was sent to Louisiana in 1751 by Louis XV, built a large town house for his family—thirteen children and a slew of in-laws and grandchildren. The adjoining town house was built some ten years later.

A flagstone carriageway leads to a First Empire parlor and the adjacent registration area; just beyond is a peaceful landscaped courtyard where a cast-iron fountain trickles into a lily pond.

The furnishings are English, French, and Louisiana antiques that proprietors Rodney and Frances Smith have collected over more than twenty-five years of travel. Handcarved four-posters, canopy beds, armoires, Oriental rugs, and comfortable wing chairs are complemented by framed contemporary works by local artists. Fabrics are custom made, the monogrammed bed linens are pure cotton percale from Egypt, and the plump pillows are down filled. Many of the baths have Jacuzzis; all feature phones and Crabtree & Evelyn toiletries.

Rooms and suites are in the two adjoining main buildings (there is a steep climb up winding stairs to the second and third floors) and in the former slave quarters off the courtyard. A private elevator leads to Rooms 30 and 33 (which are let separately or as a suite; Paul Newman took the suite option when he stayed at the Soniat during the filming of *Blaze*). Room 32 is a charmer, with a private verandah facing the courtyard. Room 28 is a large, luxurious suite with a stunning, custom-made mahogany four-poster and a balcony overlooking Chartres Street.

A concierge is on duty twenty-four hours to arrange for, say, a horsedrawn carriage to transport you to Antoine's for dinner. The parlor boasts a well-stocked honor bar, and there is a business center with fax and photocopying services.

Guests who want even more space and privacy should check out the six apartments nearby on Esplanade Avenue in Girod House, also owned by the Smiths. Furnished with antiques, the apartments have equipped kitchens with fine china, crystal, and cutlery.

Rates begin at $120 for single occupancy, semi-suites (with queen-size beds and Jacuzzi) are $115, and one-

and two-bedroom suites are $350 and $525, respectively. 1133 Chartres Street, New Orleans 70116, 504/522-0570, 800/544-8808, fax 504/522-7208. AE, MC, V.

SULLY MANSION, GARDEN DISTRICT. New Orleans architect Thomas Sully, great-nephew of the English-born portraitist of the same name, designed this wonderful Queen Anne house in 1891 for one John Rainey. Rainey occupied the house for sixteen years before moving back to his native Virginia. During the Great Depression the house changed hands no fewer than sixteen times. In 1938 it became a boardinghouse. Maralee and Jack Prigmore bought it in 1978 and changed it back to a single-family dwelling. It has been a bed-and-breakfast since 1984.

Typical of the frilly Queen Anne style, the house has a sweeping verandah, dormer windows, towers, turrets, and lovely stained-glass windows. And typical of Garden District homes, it is shaded by huge trees and surrounded by luxuriant shrubs and flowering plants. A grand piano sits in the foyer, next to a handsome carved stairway. Antique-filled rooms are large—most of them 17 by 24 feet; ceilings are 12 feet high, with crystal chandeliers dangling from ornate medallions; and doors rise up to 10 feet. Full-length windows are dressed in swag draperies, and mantels display a collection of porcelain figurines. Each of the seven guest rooms has a private bath and phone. Guests gather downstairs to chat, watch TV, or play board games. There is no swimming pool. The St. Charles Streetcar is just a block away, and Commander's Palace restaurant is a block and a half away.

Complimentary French pastries, juice, and coffee or tea are served in a formal dining room. Rates are from $85 to $150. 2631 Prytania Street, New Orleans 70130, 504/891-0457. MC, V.

Small Hotels

DAUPHINE ORLEANS. In a good French Quarter location —a block from Bourbon Street and three blocks from Canal—the Dauphine Orleans has several kinds of accommodations. Most of the rooms and suites are in the main building, which is a restoration of an eighteenth-century town house. But there are cottages sprinkled around the courtyard and pool, and across the street, tucked away behind an iron gate, small, secluded rooms surround a large patio.

Far and away the most interesting of the 109 rooms are Rooms 108, 109, and 110 in the main house. During a 1991 renovation, workers tearing away Sheetrock in those rooms discovered the original brick-between-posts structure, the same used in the earliest houses of the Creoles. That, plus the discovery of antique handforged iron nails, date the building from about 1790. (The hotel wisely opted to leave the brick-between-posts intact and visible.) Sheetrock had also obscured fireplaces and cypress-and-pine beams. In Room 108, what is now the bedroom was once a kitchen; antique cast-iron pots and pans were discovered beneath its floorboards. This suite's Jacuzzi bath, with its porcelain shell basin and brass fittings, was once a carriageway.

All of the rooms and suites have minibars, in-room safes, hair dryers, and cable TV. Beds are turned down nightly, and the morning newspaper is delivered to your door. A light complimentary breakfast is served in a cheerful room; afternoon tea is served daily; and a little van whisks guests around the downtown area. You have use of a small exercise room off the courtyard, a guest library, and valet parking in an on-site garage. There is no restaurant, but the Bagnio Lounge, so it is said, occupies a former bordello.

Singles are from $110 to $150, doubles begin at $120, patio rooms are $130 to $190, and suites run from $160 to $250. 415 Dauphine Street, New Orleans 70112, 504/586-1800, 800/521-7111, fax 504/586-1409. AE, DC, MC, V.

HOTEL MAISON DE VILLE. According to local legend, New Orleans was the birthplace not only of jazz but of the cocktail. And according to the Maison de Ville, the three-story French Quarter building that houses the hotel was the nineteenth-century home of the cocktail's creator, one Antoine Amedée Peychaud.

Peychaud or no, the Maison de Ville is one of the city's finest small hotels, with twenty-three rooms and suites in the main house, in the attached slave quarters, and in the nearby Audubon Cottages. The flavor throughout is that of a French country inn. Though rooms in the main house are quite small, they are exquisitely furnished in eighteenth- and nineteenth-century antiques; most have four-posters or canopy beds and marble-top tables. Baths have brass basins and fittings.

In the attached slave quarters (which date from the 1700s and may be among the oldest buildings in the Quarter), rooms are smaller but no less elegant, with exposed brick walls and fireplaces. Tennessee Williams lived and wrote for a time in Room 9. These rooms open onto a glorious brick courtyard that is home to lush banana trees, flowers, and a three-tiered cast-iron fountain that splashes into a fish pond. Take note of the three all-night bars just across the street and the fact that Bourbon Street hollers just a half block away. You may need earplugs to get any sleep.

The finest, quietest, and priciest accommodations are in the seven Audubon Cottages, two blocks away on Dauphine Street. Dating from about 1788, the little houses are named for John James Audubon, who lived in

Cottage No. 1 in 1821 while working on his Birds of America series. The cottage's one- and two-bedroom apartments have terra cotta floors, private patios, period furnishings, and kitchens (refrigerators are stocked with soft drinks, lemon, and mixers). The hotel's pool, available to all guests, is within this secluded section.

Whatever section you choose, your bed will be turned down each night and a foil-wrapped chocolate left on your pillow. In the morning you'll be pampered with a breakfast of fresh-squeezed juice, croissants, and a pot of coffee, which will arrive on a silver tray with the morning paper and a single rose. Room service is available from the adjacent Bistro; a concierge is at the front desk to make reservations and answer questions. If you thought to put your shoes outside your door before turning in, you'll find the polished pair there in the morning.

A single twin-bed room is $95, doubles begin at $135, and a two-bedroom cottage is $385. 727 Toulouse Street, New Orleans 70116, 504/561-5858, 800/634-1600, fax 504/561-5858, ext. 225. AE, DC, MC, V.

LAFAYETTE HOTEL. Another small hotel with a Gallic flair, the Lafayette is a modern rendition of a hotel of the same name built on this site in 1916. The colorful history of the original hotel includes its use by the U. S. Navy as a barracks for Waves during World War II. The Waves, the Navy equivalent of the army's WACs, evacuated the premises shortly after the war, and over the decades the property fell into a state of disrepair. It reopened in 1991 after a $7.5 million renovation.

The hotel is adjacent to tree-shaded Lafayette Square, is five blocks from the French Quarter, and is right on the St. Charles Streetcar line. The art galleries of the revitalizing Warehouse District are less than a five-minute walk away.

An ornate marquee overhangs the front entrance, where

a liveried doorman is on duty. The dining rooms of Mike's on the Avenue, one of the city's hottest tickets, are on each side of a small but chic foyer. A concierge sits at a polished mahogany desk opposite the registration desk.

Of the forty-four accommodations, twenty are elegant suites replete with marble wet bars and refrigerators, four of which come with Jacuzzis. Many of the rooms have four-posters and homey touches such as well-stocked bookshelves, easy chairs, and ottomans. Marble baths equipped with hair dryers, Swiss-milled soaps, cuddly terry robes, and brass fittings, in-room safes, and roomy closets with full-length mirrors are other amenities.

The hotel provides valet laundry, dry cleaning, and parking. There is neither a pool nor a fitness center, but guests get a discount at a nearby health club. Double rooms begin at $135, one-bedroom Jacuzzi suites are $185 to $350, and two-bedroom suites are $295 to $550. 600 St. Charles Avenue, New Orleans 70130, 504/524-4441, 800/733-4754, fax 504/523-7327. AE, DC, MC, V.

LE PAVILLON. The nearby Superdome was not so much as a flickering, futuristic pipe dream when the New Hotel Denechaud opened in 1907. The hotel was an international sensation, the grandest of grand hotels. Its wonders included the city's first hydraulic elevators, first basement, and—ta ta!—electric lights. After some sixty-odd years, by which time the hotel had changed hands and its interior had been extensively refurbished, a flurry of European imports included the lobby's crystal chandeliers from Czechoslovakia, marble railings from the Grand Hotel in Paris, and Italian marble for the massive columns that support the *porte cochère*. It reopened in the 1970s as Le Pavillon, and it is one of the great bargains in the CBD.

The two hundred rooms are identical in decor, though they vary in size. Those with bay windows overlooking Baronne Street are roomier, but each is done in mahogany traditional furnishings and with good-quality fabrics. The eight suites are knockouts, particularly the Antique Suite, which is awash in velvets, brocades, satins, and marble and features a dramatically draped canopy bed. There are rooms for nonsmokers and for disabled travelers.

Each day at noon the Gold Room restaurant lays out an all-you-can-eat buffet of more than sixty dishes. Other amenities include a comfortable lounge just off the lobby, good business services, a rooftop pool and sundeck, a concierge, and a parking valet. Singles are from $99 to $155; doubles, $99 to $170; and suites, $295 to $550. 833 Poydras Street, New Orleans 70140, 504/581-3111, 800/535-9095, fax 504/522-5543. AE, DC, MC, V.

THE PONTCHARTRAIN. Put simply, this is one of the best hotels in town. Elegant, dignified, and very romantic, it sits on the fringe of the Garden District. Its proximity to the city's grandest residential district is appropriate. Built in 1927 by Lysle Aschaffenburg as a luxury residential hotel, the 102-room Pontchartrain had "permanent residents" until 1990. In fact, many of the museum-quality antiques and artworks belonged to residents who subsequently left them to the hotel. And although descendants of Mr. Lysle, as he was called, sold the hotel in 1987, it still has the ambience of a family-run guesthouse. Service is swift, efficient, and friendly.

The Pontchartrain's sumptuous suites are named for the celebrity guests who frequented them, notably Charles Boyer, Richard Burton, Tyrone Power, Rod Serling, and Tennessee Williams; although Napoleon was not among the notables, the suite named in his honor is among the most dramatic. And if you forgot to pack your grand piano, not to worry; there's one in the Mary Martin Suite. No two suites (or rooms) are alike; each manages to reflect the personality of its former occupant. The Rita Hayworth Suite, with its bold colors and designs, is as glamorous as she was. Though the décor differs, each of the forty-six suites has a full kitchen or kitchenette with coffeemaker, and spacious living and dining rooms. If you happen to be staying in one of the two penthouse suites, invite sixty-five of your friends in for cocktails; no one will feel crowded.

Although the suites offer the best seats in the house—facing St. Charles Avenue—the rear rooms are little pensions that are quite moderately priced for so grand a hotel. Outfitted with queen-size beds and shower baths, they won't exactly leave you in a state of deprivation: twenty-four-hour room service, nightly turndowns, valet laundry, morning newspaper delivery, and a limo are all available, whatever the size of your digs.

This is not the place to look for pools, Nautilus equipment, and glitzy discos. However, the Caribbean Room is one of the city's best restaurants, Café Pontchartrain is a favorite breakfast spot for local uptowners, and the Bayou Bar is a piano bar of considerable notes.

Pensions are $125; standard rooms, $155 to $170; suites, $225 to $295; and penthouses, $600. 2031 St. Charles Avenue, New Orleans 70140, 504/524-0581, 800/777-6193, fax 504/529-1165. AE, DC, MC, V.

LE RICHELIEU. A nineteenth-century macaroni factory and five Greek Revival rowhouses of the same period make up this little jewel, one of the city's best buys. A pleasant, quiet retreat in the French Quarter, near Esplanade Avenue, the four-story hotel is lined with wrought-iron balconies, and dormer windows poke through the rooftop. Owner and manager Frank Rochefort, Jr. lives on the premises, and he keeps careful watch to see that everything runs smoothly.

There are eighty-eight rooms and seventeen suites, each of which is individually decorated with a keen eye for detail. Most of the rooms have walk-in closets big enough to sleep in, mirrored walls, refrigerators, hair dryers, and even full-size ironing boards (irons are available from housekeeping). Sewing kits are included in the bath amenity packets. Extra amenities in the one- and two-bedroom suites include wet bars, dining areas, and private balconies. The romantic honeymoon suite has a huge, curtained four-poster. The three-bedroom VIP suite, done in Mexican and Spanish antiques, has stucco walls, cypress floors and Oriental rugs, a stereo system, and a marble bath and steam room.

The Terrace Restaurant and Lounge overlook the pretty courtyard and pool. Breakfast is served all day and room service is available. Free on-site parking in a patrolled lot is not the least of the amenities. A small business center provides photocopying, telex, and fax services.

Standard doubles begin at $95, one-bedroom suites begin at $135, and two-bedroom suites start at $235. The McCartney Suite is $175, and the VIP suite is $425. 1234 Chartres Street, New Orleans 70116, 504/529-2492, 800/535-9653, fax 504/524-8179. AE, DC, MC, V.

The Big Hotels and Main Chains

FAIRMONT. A grand hotel in the old tradition, the Fairmont opened in 1893 as the Grunewald. In 1923 the name was changed to the Roosevelt (for Teddy, who died in 1919), and many locals still call it that (it's been the Fairmont since 1965). The Roosevelt was home away from capitol for Louisiana's controversial governor, Huey Long—who was assassinated in Baton Rouge in 1935—as it was later for his brother, Governor Earl Long. In 1927 Huey set up his campaign headquarters at the Roosevelt. When he became governor he had the ninety-mile Airline Highway built so he'd have easy access from the hotel to the capitol building in Baton Rouge. As for

Earl, he never looked so good as when portrayed by Paul Newman in the movie *Blaze*, many scenes for which were shot in the Fairmont. And the hotel was the inspiration for novelist Arthur Hailey, whose bestseller *Hotel* became a TV series. (The series was shot at the flagship Fairmont in San Francisco, but Hailey compiled notes for the book at the New Orleans hotel.)

In 1908 a subterranean nightclub called the Cave opened beneath what is now the Blue Room. Believed to have been the nation's first supper club, it was a spectacular place with waterfalls, stalactites, Ziegfeld-style showgirls, and dixieland bands. In 1935 the Blue Room itself opened, and for almost twenty years clear-channel radio station WWL broadcast music "coming to you live from the Blue Room of the Roosevelt Hotel in downtown New Orleans."

The Fairmont recently celebrated its centennial with a $22 million renovation of all 753 rooms and sixty suites. The lobby's scarlet carpeting, which was beginning to look a bit worn, has been replaced with blue, red, and gold tones. The giant crystal chandeliers, which extend through the block-long lobby from University Place to Baronne Street, remain, as do the massive gilded pillars. Rooms and suites were redecorated with new furniture and carpets and drapes in shades of blue, forest green, and gold.

The grande dame may be old, but she has many modern amenities: guest phones with voice mail and two lines, in-room computer capability, suites with fax machines (the hotel also has a full-service business center), health club, two lighted tennis courts, outdoor pool, foreign currency exchange, and cable TV with movie channels. Pampering includes cushy-soft goose-down pillows and comforters, electric shoe buffers, nightly turndowns, and oversized marble baths with tub clotheslines and big, thirsty bath towels. A concierge is on duty in the lobby, where shops include a pastry shop and a florist. Room service is available around the clock, and Bailey's is a twenty-four-hour restaurant.

The hotel's main dining room is the Sazerac, a giddily romantic room in ruby reds and white laces. The adjacent Sazerac bar is named for the nation's first cocktail, a concoction created in the French Quarter in 1859 (more about the Fairmont's restaurants and bars in Chapters 13 and 15).

Doubles are from $150 to $195, one-bedroom suites begin at $315, and two-bedroom suites start at $440. University Place, New Orleans 70140, 504/529-7111, 800/527-4727, fax 504/522-2303. AE, CB, D, DC, MC, V.

HYATT REGENCY. First things first: The Top of the Dome, the city's only revolving rooftop restaurant, has a nightly Chocoholic Bar with a menu of chocolate-dipped strawberries, chocolate fondue, white chocolate macadamia nut clusters, brownies, tortes, cakes, and mousses. Sitting 360 feet up in the air, it also offers pretty spectacular views.

Adjacent to the Superdome and connected to the New Orleans Centre shopping mall, the sprawling hotel is built around an atrium that soars to 260 feet. Eight glass-enclosed elevators glide up and down, and light pours through "space frame" windows that are 50 feet wide and 200 feet tall. A $16 million renovation in 1993 brightened up the vast reception area, adding chandeliers that are only slightly smaller than Lake Pontchartrain.

There seem to be several million restaurants, cafés, and lounges on the third-floor atrium level. There's a business center, health club, sports bar with video games, florist shop, twenty-four-hour AT&T translation services, and concierge. A complimentary shuttle scoots guests to Riverwalk, the Jax Brewery, and Canal Place.

Of the 1,184 rooms and 100 suites, 1,086 are in a

twenty-three-story high-rise and 108 are lanai rooms just off the swimming pool terrace. Extra pampering (private key access elevators, concierge, complimentary continental breakfast and afternoon hors d'oeuvres) is available in the twenty-seventh floor Regency Club. One of the Regency Club suites has an unusual four-poster crafted of pewter, and a marble bath so big it has two TVs in it. Frequent guests with children age fifteen and under can take advantage of the Camp Hyatt program, which features half-price rooms for kids and half-price children's portions in all of the restaurants.

Single rooms are $165 and doubles are $190. Regency Club singles are $190 and doubles are $215. Poydras at Loyola Avenue, New Orleans 70140, 504/561-1234, 800/233-1234, fax 504/587-4141. AE, CB, D, DC, MC, V.

LE MERIDIEN. Not the least of Le Meridien's attractions are the dixieland bands that liven things up at night in its sophisticated marble-and-brass rotunda. The France-based hotel seems quite at home in the old French Creole city. Matter of fact, the modern high-rise sits cheek to jowl with a small, almost ridiculously ornate nineteenth-century cast-iron building—and neither appears the least bit anachronistic.

Soaring thirty stories over the CBD, the Meridien is across the street from the French Quarter and a five-minute walk from the Aquarium, Canal Place, and River-walk. The 494 rooms and seven suites are sleek and spacious. Ultramodern furnishings are upholstered in fabrics of soft beiges and greys. All rooms have minibars, dual-line phones, and cable TV with movie channels. Corner split-level suites, whose two-story windows offer a sweeping view of the downtown area, have two bedrooms, with a powder room downstairs and a full bath upstairs. Room service is available twenty-four hours a day from La Gauloise, the Parisian bistro-style restaurant that serves breakfast, lunch, and dinner.

There is a rooftop pool and tanning deck, sauna, Jacuzzi, and an excellent health club, to which many locals belong, which boasts Nautilus' "Next Generation" equipment and a staff of trainers.

Doubles run from $170. Suites range from $450 for a junior one-bedroom suite to $1,500 for the two-bedroom Presidential suite. 614 Canal Street, New Orleans 70130, 504/525-6500, 800/543-4300, fax 504/586-1543. AE, CB, D, DC, MC, V.

MONTELEONE. If the Monteleone were about fifteen years older it could well have been the luxurious hotel where Rhett and Scarlett stayed on their New Orleans honeymoon. You can almost see the two strolling in the lobby beneath the blimp-sized crystal chandeliers or ensconced in one of the luscious suites. The French Quarter's oldest, tallest, most traditional hotel celebrated its one-hundredth birthday in 1986. It is still operated by descendants of Antonio Monteleone, a shoemaker who came to the Crescent City from Sicily. His boot factory was at the corner of Royal and Bienville; his eye was on the sixty-four-room Commercial Hotel across the street. In time he bought it, and over the years the little hotel was transformed into the present-day sixteen-story, six hundred-room luxury hotel with a fabulously ornate baroque facade. For decades the Monteleone was *the* place to stay in the Quarter. Other large luxury hotels have opened in the Vieux Carré, but for a whole raft of people the Monteleone is still the cat's pajamas. Even with a multi-million-dollar sprucing up in 1992, the hotel maintains its wonderful Old World charm.

But it also has twentieth-century necessities, such as the fitness center on the roof near the pool and a fully equipped business center on the mezzanine. It also has gift shops, lounges, restaurants, and—a French Quarter landmark—the revolving Carousel Bar.

Single rooms are from $115, doubles from $145, and suites from $250 to $680. 214 Royal Street, New Orleans 70140, 504/523-3341, 800/535-9595, fax 504/528-1019. AE, CB, DC, MC, V.

NEW ORLEANS HILTON RIVERSIDE & TOWERS. One of the largest and splashiest properties in this neck of the marshlands, the 1,602-room Hilton sits on a prime piece of CBD real estate: at the foot of Poydras Street, smack at the *Queen of New Orleans* riverboat landing, right on the Riverfront Streetcar line, and within a ten-minute walk of Jackson Square in the Quarter. The twenty-nine-story Towers, with such perks as white-jacketed butler service, are patterned after the Hilton's older sister, the Waldorf Towers in New York; 456 rooms and suites are in the low-rise Riverside section.

A lot goes on in this bustling hotel. The city's premier clarinetist, Pete Fountain, has his club on the third floor. It has four restaurants, seven bars, two swimming pools, a business center, and the city's best health club. The Rivercenter Racquet and Health Club has eight indoor tennis courts, three outdoor tennis courts, four racquetball courts, three squash courts, a basketball court, a golf clinic, saunas, whirlpools, a tanning bed, aerobics and exercise rooms, a unisex beauty salon, and a quarter-mile rooftop jogging path. And a masseur. There are two large parking lots, as well as a 1,600-car secured garage.

Standard singles are $210, doubles $235. An executive double runs for $255, and tower suites start at $685. 2 Poydras Street, New Orleans 70140, 504/561-0500, 800/ HILTONS, fax 504/568-1721. AE, CB, D, DC, MC, V.

OMNI ROYAL ORLEANS. For locals, this was known as the Royal O long before Omni got into the act. Almost slap in the center of the French Quarter, it's home to the Rib Room, a favorite restaurant of Orleanian movers and shakers, and to the Esplanade Lounge, a fit place for winding down after a hard day's night on the town. A mere child as these things go, the Royal O opened in 1960 on the site of the old St. Louis Hotel, a splendid place that cost a million dollars to build back in 1836; it housed not only a hotel, bar, and restaurant, but public baths and a bank. Soon after it opened, the glamorous hotel became the center of Creole social activities. In 1842 rooms in the St. Louis went for $2.50 a day and free lunches were served to noontime imbibers in the hotel's bar. During the War Between the States the St. Louis was a hospital for Confederate and Yankee soldiers alike, and during Reconstruction it was the meeting place for the Carpetbagger Legislature. The St. Louis reigned on this site until 1915, when a hurricane hit and almost completely demolished it. In the lobby of the present-day hotel is a large painting of the famous old St. Louis.

Just inside the front doors, a pair of ornate statues of Venetian Moors stand guard. The lobby is a sea of white marble, with crystal chandeliers, Oriental carpeting, and gilt-edged paintings. The rooms designed for single travelers are small, but so is the $130 price for a hotel in this prime location. All of the rooms have minibars, turndown service, and complimentary shoeshines. The suites are exotic, with four-posters canopied in delicious fabrics and enormous marble baths in bold colors (all with phones, of course); some of the suites have Jacuzzis. Many of the rooms open onto balconies trimmed in graceful wrought-iron; just bear in mind that those overlooking Royal and St. Louis Streets can be very noisy, especially during such raucous events as Mardi Gras and the Sugar Bowl.

The fitness center, pool, and La Riviera poolside restaurant are all on the roof—where, incidentally, there is a lovely, very romantic view of the French Quarter's sloping, dormered roofs. Beauty, barber, and gift shops are on the lower level.

Single rooms are $130; doubles, $155 to $250; and suites, $250 to $1,000. 621 St. Louis Street, New Orleans 70140, 504/529-5333, 800/THE-OMNI, fax 504/529-7089. AE, CB, DC, MC, V.

ROYAL SONESTA. The Sonesta sits right on one of the busiest blocks of hurly-burly Bourbon Street, but once you step into the spacious pink marble lobby you're in another world. And a serene world it is, with softly gurgling fountains, banks of lush green plants, and crystal chandeliers and sconces. The courtyard, tucked away from the street noises, is a delightful place filled with orange trees, palms, flowering plants, and umbrella tables. (If you can't wrench yourself away from the sights and sounds of Bourbon, take one of the front rooms with a balcony. If you want to sleep, you'll fare better with a balcony room that overlooks the courtyard.)

Reproductions of nineteenth-century furnishings and attractive pastel fabrics create a country French ambience. But of course the five hundred rooms and suites have all manner of modern conveniences: stocked minibars, cable TV with more than a hundred movie channels, and phones with speakers, voice mail, teleconferencing capabilities, and hookups for fax machines and modems. If you left your computer in your other purse, you can rent one in the business center and make use of its fax, photocopying, and secretarial services. Elegant suites range from petites to split-levels to two-bedroom-two-bath, and all have wet bars. On the seventh floor concierge level are further perks: key-activated elevator, concierge, complimentary morning coffee and pastries, afternoon cocktails, bath phones, hair dryers, and such.

The hotel's two restaurants are Begue's, a dress-up

place for Continental cuisine, and the Desire Oyster Bar, which dishes up po' boys and salads as well as oysters. A trio entertains in the Mystick Den, a dixieland band jazzes things up in the Can Can Café, and drinks are knocked back in several other bars. And after all that dining and imbibing, you can work out in the exercise room and swim in the heated outdoor pool.

Singles are from $130 to $200 and doubles from $140 to $235. Concierge rooms begin at $205 and suites start at $260. 300 Bourbon Street, New Orleans 70140, 504/586-0300, 800/SONESTA, fax 504/586-0335. AE, CB, D, DC, MC, V.

WESTIN CANAL PLACE. Far and away, the most sweeping view of the river, the CBD, and the French Quarter is from the thirtieth-floor rooftop pool and sundeck of the Westin. But then the entire hotel is designed with views in mind. The lavish lobby, which sits on the eleventh floor of the Canal Place mall, has two-story arched windows as well as miles of rose Carrara marble, eighteenth- and nineteenth-century artworks, and greenery overflowing the massive urns. It is a fit place to sip tea and nibble scones while watching the Mississippi roll toward the Gulf of Mexico.

There are 438 rooms, including forty-one suites with one or two bedrooms. Each is done in either soft peach, green, or rose and has a marble foyer, stocked minibar, big marble baths with many amenities, phones with call-waiting, and fine European furnishings. TVs—with movie and sports channels—are tucked away in handsome armoires. The two Executive Club floors provide extra perks such as a cushy lounge, continental breakfast, and afternoon hors d'oeuvres. Fitness facilities are right beneath your feet at Racquetball One in Canal Place, as are beauty salons. And of course you can roam the fifty or so shops in the mall.

The Westin's restaurant, Le Jardin, serves regional and Continental cuisine and provides twenty-four-hour room service. Sunday brunch, replete with toe-tapping live jazz, is a fun affair. The Westin has a multilingual staff, a currency exchange, and a twenty-four-hour AT&T language line that sorts out more than 125 languages. The hotel provides valet parking and there is a nine-story parking garage in the mall.

Rates range from $180 for a single to $625 for a suite. 100 Iberville Street, New Orleans 70130, 504/566-7006, 800/228-3000, fax 504/553-5133. AE, CB, DC, MC, V.

Other large downtown chains that offer a full range of cafés, restaurants, lounges, pools, and fitness and business centers are the Sheraton New Orleans (500 Canal Street, New Orleans 70130, 504/525-2500, 800/325-3535, fax 504/561-0178; doubles from $200), the Marriott New Orleans (555 Canal Street, New Orleans 70140, 504/581-1000, 800/228-9290, fax 504/581-5790; doubles from $205), the Inter-Continental (444 St. Charles Avenue, New Orleans 70130, 504/525-5566, 800/332-4246, fax 504/523-7310; doubles from $180), and the Clarion (1500 Canal Street, New Orleans 70112, 504/522-4500, 800/824-3359; fax 504/525-2644; doubles from $117).

Chapter Thirteen
♦♦♦♦♦♦♦♦♦♦♦♦♦
Restaurants

EVERYTHING in New Orleans revolves around food. The thought of having a board meeting, committee meeting, press conference, or *any* gathering without at the very least an array of canapés is, well, unthinkable. No one knows when the local fixation on food took root. It may very well hark back to the earliest days of the colony, when the eighteenth-century Creoles ate, drank, and attempted to be merry in the face of floods, hurricanes, yellow fever, and all manner of hardships. In any case, Orleanians love to eat and to dine out. Many locals make a clear distinction between "eating out" and "dining out," and those who do disdain the former in favor of the latter. Dining out is done in the leisurely European style, in which going to a restaurant is the evening's entertainment and not an appetizer for, say, the theater or the opera. And, typically, visitors to the city are not asked, "What have you done since you've been here?" but "Where have you eaten?"

If there's one thing the average Orleanian likes better than dining out, it's talking about food—or, to be more precise, arguing about food. These things being highly subjective, no one is going to win a debate about where you can get the best shrimp Creole or bananas Foster or which little dive turns out the best po' boys. But such discussions seem to be in the local genes.

The Crescent City has fine old-line restaurants such as Antoine's and Tujague's that have been around for well over a century, and famed, firmly established places such as K-Paul's, Commander's Palace, Galatoire's, Arnaud's, and Brennan's. Apart from K-Paul's, whose celebrity chef Paul Prudhomme serves an embellished version of Cajun cooking, all of the aforementioned eateries are French Creole or a blend of it. French Creole dishes, which originated in the city, are identifiable by rich, rich sauces. Cajun cooking, often called the country cousin of citified Creole, relies more on hot spices and herbs and tends to be more robust.

Although the French Creole influence remains strong, in the past few years a new breed of hot young chefs has burst on the scene and taken the city by storm. Several of them—notably Emeril Lagasse, who has two popular restaurants—used to work at Commander's Palace, a veritable training ground for new restaurateurs. (Paul Prudhomme was executive chef at Commander's before he opened K-Paul's in 1979.) Contemporary Creole is a label often attached to their imaginative offerings, but chef Susan Spicer of Bayona trumps them with her "New World" appellation.

You can't really talk about New Orleans restaurants without mentioning the Brennan family. The original Brennan's on Royal Street was founded in 1946 by six Brennan siblings. In 1974, four Brennans—including Ella, whom locals consider a culinary icon—left the eponymous French Quarter bastion and opened the prestigious Commander's Palace in the Garden District. Since that time Miss Ella, as she is called, has been the guiding force behind the highly successful restaurants that have been opened by sundry Brennan offspring. The first was Mr. B.'s Bistro (the Mr. B is Ella's nephew Ralph, who operates the restaurant with his sister, Cindy), followed by the Palace Café and Bacco. The opening of a new Brennan's restaurant is always eagerly anticipated by Orleanians.

New Orleans is not in a foreign country, but there are several menu items that can be baffling to first-time visitors. Although waiters here are accustomed to describing and explaining dishes to tourists, the following culinary lexicon may give you a leg up.

♦ *Andouille*—spicy Cajun pork sausage

♦ *Bananas Foster*—a dessert of bananas sautéed in butter, brown sugar, cinnamon, and banana liqueur, flamed tableside with white rum, and served over vanilla ice cream

♦ *Barbecued shrimp*—Forget about Memphis-style barbecue. This dish consists of shrimp boiled in their shells and served in a garlic sauce. You tuck a bib around your neck, roll up your sleeves, ask for more napkins, and peel 'n' eat the critters.

♦ *Beignet*—a holeless doughnut similar to a cruller that is swathed in powdered sugar; the term also applies to appetizers such as fried crawfish or redfish

♦ *Café au lait*—a potent half-and-half blend of hot chicory coffee and hot milk

♦ *Café brulot*—after-dinner coffee blended with spices, orange peel, and sugar, flamed with brandy, and served in special cups

♦ *Chicory*—an herb, the roots of which are dried, ground, roasted, and used to flavor coffee

- *Courtbouillon*—spicy stew made with fish fillets, tomatoes, onions, and mixed vegetables

- *Crawfish*—Elsewhere called crawdads or crayfish, this diminutive crustacean is also known locally as a mudbug because it makes its home in the mud of freshwater streams.

- *Dressed*—In New Orleans sandwich shops this term has to do with what you want on your sandwich. If it's "dressed," it wears mayonnaise, lettuce, and tomato.

- *Étouffée*—Crawfish and/or shrimp *étouffée* crop up on almost every menu in town. *Étouffée* is the French word for "smothered"; the sea critters are "smothered" in a thick, spicy sauce.

- *Filé*—ground sassafras leaves used for seasoning

- *Gumbo*—a thick, robust soup, always made with rice and often with okra, filé, andouille, chicken, or seafood

- *Jambalaya*—A distant kin of Spanish *paella*, this dish is made with yellow rice, spices, bits of andouille, along with seafood, ham, shrimp, tomatoes—variations abound.

- *Mirliton*—a vegetable pear

- *Muffuletta*—A hefty concoction served between huge slices of Italian bread, this sandwich is made with Italian meats and cheese and liberal portions of olive salad.

- *Plantain*—a kind of banana that is served fried, simmered in sherry, or prepared like candied yams

- *Po' boy*—in other places known as a hero or a sub. The New Orleans rendition consists of crisp French bread stuffed with almost anything you can imagine: roast beef, ham, fried oysters, whatever.

♦ *Praline*—a sweet, sweet candy patty made with sugar, butter, and pecans. It's hard to leave town without a few boxes tucked away in your suitcase.

During the summer months you can often stroll into even the most famous restaurant and be seated without a reservation—unless a major convention happens to be in town. Reservations are highly recommended if you plan to be in town between September and May, and they are essential, and should be made well in advance, for full-house events such as Mardi Gras, the Sugar Bowl, and Jazz Fest.

In recent years waiters in a few lesser-known restaurants have slyly tacked on a 15 percent gratuity while neglecting to mention that they've done so. Be sure to examine your bill to see that you're not tipping on top of a tip. Also, New Orleans waiters expect a tip based on the total tab, including the 9 percent tax, drinks, and wine—a fact that becomes apparent when you see that your credit card ticket shows only the total. Apart from those caveats, tipping in New Orleans is the same as it is for the rest of the country: 20 percent for a luxury restaurant and 15 percent for moderate and inexpensive places (and, of course, figure your tip based on the service you've received).

More than fifteen hundred restaurants line the metropolitan area. Lengthy though it is, our listing is still highly selective. It's hard to find really bad food in New Orleans, although any restaurant anywhere can have a bad night. Several restaurants offer an early-bird special; if you're interested in having dinner as early as 5:30 or 6:00, you can do so at a considerable savings. Policies change from season to season, so check the restaurant of your choice to find out about specials as well as its current credit card policy.

Our prices are based on entrées only, for one person,

exclusive of the 9 percent tax, gratuity, and beverages.
But remember that the city is awash with à la carte menus
and that a few little extras such as appetizer, veggies, and
dessert will knock the price right out of our ball park.
With that in mind, we call $25 and above "expensive,"
$10 and below "inexpensive," and everything in between
"moderate." Dress is casual unless specified otherwise.
The telephone area code for all listings is 504, and
standard abbreviations are used for credit cards.

Highly Recommended

ANTOINE'S. In the opening pages of her 1948 mystery
Dinner at Antoine's, Frances Parkinson Keyes describes a
dinner party that takes place in the venerable French
Creole restaurant. (Antoine's is not only the oldest restaurant in New Orleans but the oldest continuously operated
family-run restaurant in the country). Two true-life characters in the novel are then proprietor Roy Alciatore,
grandson of the founder, and his cousin Angelo, who is
also maitre d'. In 1899 Antoine's originated Oysters
Rockefeller, a dish so rich it was named for John D.
Rockefeller, at that time the richest man in the world.
Another Antoine's original, this one concocted by the
founder's son Jules, is *pompano en papillote*. Created in
honor of a visit to the restaurant by a famous French
balloonist, the idea was to prepare a dish that resembled
the balloon. The result was a filet of fish in white wine,
baked in a paper bag that "ballooned" in the oven.

The fifteen-room restaurant remains much as Keyes
described it, but the present-day, fifth-generation proprietor, Bernard (Randy) Guste, has made a couple of significant changes during his watch. The first innovation,
which appeared in 1991, was English subtitles on the
menu. Soon after, the restaurant presented a moderately
priced luncheon menu which happens to be an excellent

buy: a four-course lunch goes for less than $20. Alligator bisque, creole gumbo, *noisettes d'agneau Alciatore*, and baked Alaska are just some of the Antoine's specialties. The coffee, a dark French roast, is strong enough to stand alone, but it contains no chicory. After your meal, try to muster up the strength to waddle around to see the dining rooms and peer into the twenty-five-thousand-bottle wine cellar. Any local will tell you to make your first visit to Antoine's with someone who's well acquainted with the restaurant, that is, someone who has a regular waiter. The staff caters to regular customers and sometimes treats unfamiliar diners indifferently.

713 St. Louis Street, French Quarter. 581-4422. Closed Sunday. Reservations and jackets required for dinner. Moderate to expensive. AE, CB, DC, MC, V.

ANACAPRI. Named for the birthplace of chef/owner Andrea Apuzzo, Anacapri is a lovely restaurant whose walls are painted with scenes of the Blue Grotto, the Faraglioni rocks, and other famous landmarks of the romantic Isle of Capri. Andrea's cuisine is a happy marriage of regional ingredients, such as tasso, crawfish, and oysters, and his homemade pasta, imported Italian rice, and heavenly sauces. Wine is served by the glass, and includes Italian and California labels. Anacapri is a newcomer, having opened in the French Quarter in 1993, but Andrea's in Metairie (3100 19th Street, 834-8583) opened several years ago and is still going strong. Despite its suburban location, Andrea's tends to be a bit more formal than Anacapri, though neither eatery is the place for jeans and cutoffs.

320 Bienville Street, Bienville House Hotel, French Quarter. 522-9056. Open daily for breakfast, lunch, and dinner. Reservations suggested for dinner. Moderate. AE, DC, MC, V.

ARNAUD'S. Arnaud's is a delightfully romantic restaurant that serves superb French Creole cuisine. In the main dining room ceiling fans silently revolve high above mosaic tile floors, etched glass, and masses of potted palms and ferns. The à la carte menu highlights the house specialties: shrimp Arnaud, turtle soup, trout meunière, and filet of pompano served *en croûte* are standouts among the sea creatures; winners in the fowl category include stuffed quail and roast duck à l'orange; beef Wellington, rack of lamb for two, and steak *au poivre* are all good meat choices; and for dessert the bananas Foster is marvelous. And don't forget that the Sunday jazz brunch, with a mellow jazz trio, is one of the best in town.

Before you leave, go up to the second floor to see the Germaine Wells Mardi Gras Museum. The late Mrs. Wells, who died in the 1980s, was the daughter of restaurant founder Arnaud Cazenave and the queen of more Mardi Gras balls than anyone else in history. The museum displays an array of crowns and scepters along with all of Mrs. Wells' sequined and beaded Carnival gowns—except for the one in which she chose to be buried. Admission to the museum is free.

813 Bienville Street, French Quarter. 523-5433. Open daily for lunch and dinner. Reservations advised for dinner. Jacket and tie preferred. Moderate to expensive. AE, CB, DC, MC, V.

BACCO. The several handsome, high-ceilinged rooms of Ralph and Cindy Brennan's Italian restaurant feature such *luxe* touches as chandeliers made with hand-painted Venetian silk, a star-studded ceiling, and a stunning mural of Bacchus, the Roman god of wine. Bacco's menu offers northern and southern Italian dishes from Milan to Sicily. The pasta is homemade, and there is a wood-burning fireplace from which several delicious dishes emerge.

310 Chartres Street, Hotel de la Poste, French Quarter. 522-2426. Open daily for breakfast, lunch, and dinner. Reservations and jackets advised for dinner. Moderate to expensive. AE, CB, DC, MC, V.

BAYONA. A renovated creole cottage on a quiet French Quarter street houses Susan Spicer's hot-ticket bistro. *Trompe l'oeil* murals of Mediterranean scenes decorate the walls and fresh flowers add to the cheerful atmosphere. When it's crowded, as it often is, the restaurant can be quite noisy. Susan's "New World" cuisine is difficult to categorize. Expect the unexpected: Things like grapes, raspberries, and spiced pecans crop up in the least likely places, adding tasty surprises.

430 Dauphine Street, French Quarter. 525-4455. Closed Sunday and at noon on Saturday. Reservations advised. Moderate. AE, MC, V.

BRENNAN'S. Brennan's home is a twelve-room town house that was called Casa Faurie when it was built in 1795 for a Spaniard named José Faurie. The historic building also housed the Banque de la Louisiane—you can see the initials LB worked into the wrought-iron balcony rail. When the bank went belly up, it again became a private home. In the mid-nineteenth century it was the home of world chess champion Paul Morphy.

When the Brennan family opened this restaurant in 1946 and brought back the old Creole custom of a "second breakfast," breakfast at Brennan's became internationally acclaimed—though we Anglos call this kind of breakfast brunch. Alas, the one thing lacking is the leisurely nineteenth-century pace. This is a very busy place, and even with reservations you'll probably have to wait. Happily, there are plenty of tables in the lavish courtyard.

Dinner, too, is an elegant affair. There is both an à la carte and a *table d'hôte* menu; the latter leans more on seafood entrees, and the former features several steaks as well as veal and lamb dishes. The restaurant has a good wine list that includes French, Australian, and California labels.

417 Royal Street, French Quarter. 525-9711. Open daily at 8:00 A.M. Reservations essential. Jackets are preferred for dinner. Very expensive. AE, CB, DC, MC, V.

BOZO'S. Arguably the best seafood restaurant in town and unquestionably one of the most popular, Bozo's has been operated by the Vodanovich family since 1928. It's a good place to bring the kids; the ambience is nothing if not casual, and plates for children under twelve are available for any dish on the menu. Try the oyster bar or the chicken andouille gumbo to get things going. Catfish and shrimp come fried or broiled; crab is stuffed; and the same kinds of critters turn up in sandwiches and po' boys. There are several combo platters that take in just about everything. Cognacs and a short but serviceable list of California wines are available, and the house wine can be ordered by the glass.

3117 Twenty-first Street, Metairie. 831-8666. Closed Sunday and Monday. No reservations. Inexpensive. MC, V.

BRIGTSEN'S. Some of the city's best South Louisiana cooking is done in this small, intimate cottage, just a stone's throw from the uptown bend in the river. Although it isn't elaborate, the tables are covered with white cloths and decorated with little vases of fresh flowers. Owner and chef Frank Brigtsen (pronounced Brightsen), a protegé of Paul Prudhomme, turns out dishes that blend Creole and Cajun influences. The menu is not lengthy and it changes daily, but look for things like Brigtsen's rendition of oysters Rockefeller (it's a wonderful, creamy soup) and roast duck served with honey-pecan sauce and dirty rice. The good selection of desserts includes homemade ice cream.

723 Dante Street, uptown. 861-7610. Open daily for dinner only. Reservations advised. Moderate to expensive. AE, MC, V.

CARIBBEAN ROOM. The main restaurant of the Pontchartrain Hotel in the Garden District is a *très intime* room in hues of rose and green; the decor, replete with richly upholstered Louis XIV-style furnishings, is as close to an upper-crust drawing room as a hotel dining room is likely to get. In 1993 a new chef came on board, but the menu will retain such dishes as grilled swordfish steak topped with a watermelon and pineapple salsa, marinated and grilled duck breast served with grilled apples and a Calvados sauce, snapper Eugene (a Caribbean tradition), and its famous mile high pie.

2031 St. Charles Avenue, Pontchartrain Hotel, Garden District. 524-0581. Closed for lunch Saturday; Sunday brunch served. Reservations and jackets required. Expensive. AE, CB, DC, MC, V.

COMMANDER'S PALACE. Consistently top rated, everything about Commander's Palace is just right: the late-nineteenth-century Victorian house, the several attractive dining rooms, the weekend jazz brunches, and of course the food. Emile Commander opened the original place in 1883. In 1974 Ella, Dottie, Dick, and John Brennan opened their rendition of Commander's Palace, serving Contemporary Creole cuisine. You won't really go wrong here, whatever your choice; standouts are fresh trout in a buttery pecan sauce and fresh lump crabmeat. Commander's also has a strong lineup of desserts.

1403 Washington Avenue, Garden District. 899-8221.

Open daily. Reservations recommended for dinner and brunch. Jackets required for dinner. Expensive. AE, CB, DC, MC, V.

EMERIL'S. When Emeril Lagasse left his kitchen at Commander's Palace in 1990 to strike out on his own, New Orleanians were virtually feverish in anticipation of the new opening. Emeril's is housed in an abandoned warehouse; exposed pipes, adobe brick walls, high ceilings, and hardwood floors are all part of its decor. The ambience is noisy, but Emeril's devotees are oblivious to the clatter and chatter. It is by now a cliché to say that every edible item in the restaurant is homemade: the goat cheese, the Worcestershire sauce, the andouille, the ice cream, the pastas. Most items are spicy enough to really wake up your taste buds.

  800 Tchoupitoulas Street, Warehouse District. 528-9393. Closed for lunch Saturday and for all meals Sunday. Reservations recommended. Jackets preferred. Moderate to expensive. AE, DC, MC, V.

GALATOIRE'S. Opened in 1905, Galatoire's is the epitome of the New Orleans French Creole restaurant. With decor that resembles a Parisian bistro, it is considered the city's best restaurant by many old-line Orleanians as well as Quarterites who rarely venture outside the boundaries of the original colony. Each Sunday afternoon is devoted to a salon during which the regulars gather to gossip and feast on their favorite foods. The menu runs several pages and includes an array of veal, steak, seafood, and chicken dishes. The French bread here is exceptionally good.

  209 Bourbon Street, French Quarter. 525-2021. Closed Monday. No reservations; arrive either early or late for lunch to avoid long lines. Jackets and ties required after 5:00 and all day Sunday; no jeans or shorts. Moderate. AE, MC, V.

GAUTREAU'S. Keep a sharp eye out for Gautreau's. Not only does it have no sign, but it's almost closeted behind trees. The restaurant closed for a short time in 1989 and then reopened; the current chef is a young California native named Richard Benz, who has once again set the place on fire—so to speak. The ground floor, which once housed a pharmacy, still has the original polished wood apothecary cabinet, which now holds wines and liquors. The cuisine is nouvelle Creole. The menu changes daily but you'll usually find good roast chicken, superbly pre-pared steaks, and crabcakes with black beans and cilantro tartare.

1728 Soniat Street, uptown. 899-7397. Dinner only, closed Sunday. Reservations advised. Moderate to expensive. MC, V.

GRILL ROOM. This is one of the city's finest restaurants. Certainly the surroundings are luxurious: The Grill Room is the main dining room of the Windsor Court Hotel, which is known for its priceless art collection. The center-piece of the dining room's marbled foyer is an exquisite Lalique table, said to be valued at $25,000. Seating is in elegantly upholstered chairs and cushy banquettes, and service is swift and efficient. Chef Kevin Graham, a 1993 inductee into the *Nation's Restaurant News* Fine Dining Hall of Fame, has put together a "Degustation"—a "sam-pling" menu—that changes twice weekly and might fea-ture such entrées as grilled tournedos of beef and foie gras, steak tartare, penne with grilled pancetta and sage, or cream of Perigord truffle with rice. Sommelier Erin White sees to the accompanying wines (the Grill Room has a superb wine cellar).

300 Gravier Street, Windsor Court Hotel, CBD. 523-6000. Open daily. Reservations essential. Jackets advised. Expensive. AE, CB, DC, MC, V.

K-PAUL'S LOUISIANA KITCHEN. A Cajun himself, born in the heart of Acadiana, Paul Prudhomme has created his own unique style: Based on the foods he grew up on (and greatly embellished), it may not be exactly authentic to his Cajun cousins, but it is wonderful. A great ambassador for New Orleans and South Louisiana, Chef Paul often takes his show on the road, and people in cities all over the globe have had the good fortune to sample his fare. New Orleanians traditionally shunned his famous eatery because of the "no reservations" and "share-a-table" policies. Happily for the locals, the rules have been changed; reservations are now accepted for dinner (but not lunch). The menu changes daily, but you can count on great gumbo, marvelous homemade breads (don't miss the corn-flour biscuits), crawfish *étouffée*, and black-eyed yellowfin tuna. The sweet potato pecan pie is a standout.

416 Chartres Street, French Quarter. 524-7394. Closed Sunday. Reservations (available for dinner only) strongly advised. Expensive. AE.

LA PROVENCE. About an hour's drive from the city, nestled in the piney woods of St. Tammany Parish on the North Shore of Lake Pontchartrain, La Provence is a romantic French restaurant that can fool you into believing you're dining in a tavern somewhere in the south of France. Cooking accoutrements hang over open fireplaces; waitresses are gowned in French provincial dress; and the ambience is warm and inviting. The restaurant, which turned twenty in 1992, is owned by Chef Chris Kerageorgiou, who was born in Port Saint Louis, Provence. As soon as you're settled in, your waitress will bring to the table a pâté that's so good you might be tempted to raid the kitchen for more. But eat lightly, because there is much wonderful food ahead of you.

On LA 190, North Shore, seven miles east of the Lake Pontchartrain causeway. 626-7662. Closed Monday and

Tuesday and Sunday night. Reservations advised. Jackets preferred. Expensive. AE, MC, V.

MR. B's BISTRO. The first of Ralph and Cindy Brennan's restaurants opened in 1979 (the Mr. B being Ralph). This is a handsome bistro, with potted palms, white-clothed tables, banquettes backed by etched-glass panels, and broad bay windows dressed in lacy café curtains. Mr. B's has a grill and hickory and pecan logs for preparing its numerous fine dishes, the best known of which is gumbo ya ya, made with a dark, burnt *roux* and thick chunks of chicken and andouille. There's a festive jazz brunch every Sunday.

201 Royal Street, French Quarter. 523-2078. Open daily. Reservations advised for dinner. Moderate. AE, CB, DC, MC, V.

MOSCA'S. A trip to Mosca's calls for about a half-hour drive to the West Bank and a sharp eye: Look for the dimly lit rustic roadhouse (it appears to be abandoned) on the left-hand side of the road. Italian/Creole food has been served in this setting since 1946, when Provino and Lisa Mosca opened the place. Mosca's menu is as unembellished as the restaurant itself. Hidden behind the stark proclamations of spaghetti, Italian shrimp, chicken, quail, and Cornish hens are marvelous ingredients, with garlic doing star turns and olive oil a strong supporting player. Oysters Mosca, served in a casserole rather than on the half shell, put the restaurant on the map. Mosca's has a strong list of Italian wines. Opening and closing hours tend to be somewhat whimsical, particularly in the summer, and you'll probably have to wait regardless of whether you have reservations. 4137 LA 90, near Waggaman on the West Bank. 436-9942. Open for dinner only; closed Sunday and Monday. Reservations advised. Inexpensive to expensive. No credit cards.

NOLA. NOLA stands for New Orleans, LA; you'll sometimes see it written Nola. No matter; Emeril Lagasse's entry in the French Quarter is in a sleek, almost spare contemporary setting and has seating on several levels. If anything, the menu here is even more imaginative than at his Warehouse District place, Emeril's. The NOLA mixed grill combines *boudin* (Cajun pork sausage), andouille, grilled chicken, and rabbit and is served with corn *maque choux* (a tasty Cajun dish made of corn, onions, and peppers), Southern cooked greens, and homemade Worcestershire sauce. An excellent choice in the seafood category is cedar plank-roasted trout with a citrus horseradish crust. It almost goes without saying that all of the desserts are homemade.

534 St. Louis Street, French Quarter. 522-6652. NOLA opens daily at 2:30 and stays open until midnight. Reservations advised for dinner. Moderate. AE, CB, DC, MC, V.

PALACE CAFÉ. Another Brennan family winner, the Palace is in a historic baroque building that dates from just after the turn of the century. The Brennans' 1990 renovation resulted in a New Orleans rendition of a Parisian grand café. It's a big, boisterous, noisy place with drugstore tiles and crowded tables and booths downstairs and a handsome staircase winding to the second level, which features a colorful mural. The food, which blends Creole with Cajun and "new New Orleans," bears the magical, typically imaginative Brennan touches. Try the oyster "shooters," Cajun *maque choux*, and the ravioli of rabbit in piquante sauce. The sweet potato cakes (served as an appetizer with grilled andouille) are marvelous. The dessert that has become a legend in its own sauce is white chocolate bread pudding.

605 Canal Street, CBD. 523-1661. Open daily for lunch and dinner. Dinner reservations advised. Moderate. CB, DC, MC, V.

PRALINE CONNECTION. On the fringe of the Quarter, in Faubourg Marigny, this tiny twelve-table spot is named for the connecting candy store in the rear. The food served here is what New Orleanians call soul Creole and what folks in more southern Southern cities call Southern. Standouts are crisp, crunchy, delicious fried chicken; succulent and spicy barbecue ribs; homestyle meatloaf; and a slew of vegetables that includes collard and mustard greens, crowder peas (alas, no black-eyed peas), and melt-in-your-mouth sweet potatoes. The cornbread is the best in town. This place is ridiculously inexpensive and the food is outstanding.

542 Frenchmen Street, Faubourg Marigny. 943-3934. Open daily for breakfast, lunch, and dinner. Reservations not accepted. Inexpensive. AE, CB, D, DC, MC, V.

THE SAZERAC. The main dining room of the Fairmont Hotel is a grand and marvelously schmaltzy place all done up in plush red velvet, shimmering chandeliers, and white lace. At dinner pianist Hugh Clay plays romantic tunes and Broadway hits. In the Fairmont's 1993 face-lift, some changes have been made in the Sazerac's menu, but signature dishes remain—lobster bisque, turtle soup, steak tartare, and rack of baby lamb. Service is done in the traditional European style, and it's a treat to watch the tableside preparations, especially of the flambéed cherries jubilee. This is one of the city's premier restaurants, and, happily, the hotel has remembered the old bromide: If it ain't broke, don't fix it.

University Place, CBD. 529-7111. Closed Sunday for lunch. Jackets and reservations required for dinner. Expensive. AE, DC, MC, V.

UPPERLINE. Set in three rooms of a nineteenth-century house, Upperline's walls are decorated with proprietor JoAnn Clevenger's private collection of works by local

artists. Executive chef Tom Cowman frequently puts together "sampling" menus. His Creole-*cum*-Cajun "Taste
of New Orleans" included samples of a shrimp and
andouille appetizer, blackened redfish, chicken *étouffée*,
barbecue shrimp, and pecan pie, at the remarkable (1993)
price of $22.50. Things tend to be on the spicy side here
—if you're not one who likes it hot, approach the jalapeño
cornbread with caution—and garlic is used with great
panache.

1413 Upperline Street, uptown. 891-9822. Open daily
for dinner only. Reservations recommended. Moderate to
expensive. AE, DC, MC, V.

OTHER EATERIES WELL WORTH A VISIT. *Alex Patout's
Louisiana Restaurant* (221 Royal Street, French Quarter,
525-7788) serves authentic South Louisiana dishes in a
stylish setting; open for dinner only. At *Bella Luna* (914
N. Peters Street, French Quarter, 529-1583) you get a
superb view of the river along with Continental cuisine;
open for dinner only, closed Sunday. *La Louisiane* (725
Iberville Street, French Quarter, 523-4664), on the scene
since 1881, is a stunning restaurant serving French Creole
and Continental specialties; lunch and dinner Monday–
Friday and dinner only Saturday and Sunday. *The Rib
Room* (Omni Royal Orleans Hotel, 621 St. Louis Street,
French Quarter, 529-7045) has an open rotisserie turning
out roast beef and fowl; a favorite meeting place of
business people. The *Bon Ton* (401 Magazine Street,
CBD, 524-3386) is an informal, cozy Cajun place. *Mike's
on the Avenue* (Lafayette Hotel, 628 St. Charles Avenue,
CBD, 523-1709) is a popular place that mixes southwestern flavors with South Louisiana ingredients.

Local Color

In addition to "dining out," most locals also like to "eat
out" in the casual country-kitchen cafés and restaurants

that abound in this town. They range from the spotless to the seemingly unsanitary, but the food is invariably good. When packing for a New Orleans trip, you might want to throw in some clothes with expandable waists.

ACME OYSTER HOUSE. The only thing fancy about the Acme is the dexterity of the oyster shuckers; they have to stay busy because Orleanians are stacked up at the bar in eager anticipation. Locals down untold numbers of raw oysters, and this is one of the favored spots for doing so. Cold beer is the proper accompaniment.

724 Iberville Street, French Quarter. 522-5973. Open daily. No reservations. Inexpensive. No credit cards.

HUMMINGBIRD GRILL. The Hummingbird's slogan, "Where the elite meet to eat," may give you pause when you first step into this all-night skid-row greasy spoon. However, after you've blinked and regained your equilibrium you will see an array of characters that includes upper-crust gents in three-piece suits and well-dressed women among the grungy street people. The daily hot-plate specials are under $4 (the menu is peppered with admonishments of "No substitutions!"). If you happen in on, say, a Monday, you'll have a choice of liver and onions, meatloaf, or "old-fashioned redbeans." After midnight come the breakfast specials. The service is invariably friendly and the food is down-home delicious. (The Hummingbird Grill is on the ground floor of a flophouse. A sign at the cash register advises that rooms are available for $23—not to be taken as a recommendation.)

804 St. Charles Avenue, CBD. 523-9165. Open twenty-four hours, every day. No reservations. Ridiculously inexpensive. No credit cards.

NAPOLEON HOUSE. Since knocking back a few adult beverages and savoring the city's romantic legends are two of the most popular local pastimes, it's only fitting that one of the city's most cherished drinking establishments is in a legendary house. Taking first things first, the bar is a rather grungy place. But for some reason—and let's not analyze these things—this is one of the most romantic places in the world when a driving rain beats on the pavement and the *1812 Overture* thunders through the bar. There is a limited menu of po' boys, muffulettas (which are served warm), and Italian ice cream, and an adjacent room has a small salad bar. People do actually eat in the Napoleon House, but its primary function is as a weathered, time-honored watering hole. If a place can be said to have charisma, then the Napoleon House has it.

As for the house legend, Napoleon Bonaparte, no doubt a charismatic kind of guy, had a host of admirers in New Orleans, not the least of whom was Nicholas Girod, the city's mayor and this house's occupant. When the Little Corporal was shipped off to St. Helena in exile, Girod and some of his cronies laid plans to rescue him and bring him to New Orleans. The third floor of Girod's house was meant to be the former emperor's new home. Napoleon passed away before he could be spirited away, however, and the plot died of natural causes. His memory lingers on here; the bar is a big draw not only for locals and tourists but for celebrities. (Kevin Costner shot some *JFK* scenes here and John Goodman and Dick Cavett are just a couple of stellar regulars who visit when they're in town.)

500 Chartres Street, French Quarter. 524-9752. Open daily. No reservations. Inexpensive. AE, MC, V.

R&O's. Bucktown, a little fishing village nestled on the banks of Lake Pontchartrain, has several simple no-frills restaurants. R&O's is one of the best. You'll see lots of locals seated at the unembellished tables or standing in line waiting for takeout. There's a good lineup of po' boys, salads, soups, pizzas, seafood platters, spaghetti and meatballs (no pastas in this place), veal parmesan, and lasagna. The garlic bread is divine.

216 Old Hammond Highway, Metairie. 831-1248. Closed for lunch on Sunday. No reservations. Inexpensive. No credit cards.

ROCKY AND CARLO'S. In Italy the *tavolo caldo* (literally, "hot table") is a fast-food joint in which you stand in line at a glass display counter, point at what you want (unless you happen to speak the lingo), pay for it, grab a handful of utensils, and eat at a table decorated with shakers of salt, pepper, and parmesan. Rocky and Carlo's is in Chalmette, about five miles from the French Quarter, but its heart is in the homeland. It's a working-class restaurant with not a frill in sight, but the food is great. The macaroni and cheese is thick and creamy, the roast beef po' boys properly sloppy, and the general ambience properly noisy and chaotic.

613 W. St. Bernard Highway, Chalmette. 279-8323. Open daily for lunch and dinner. No reservations. Inexpensive. No credit cards.

THE SADDLERY. This corner café is actually called Miss Jean's, but the "Saddlery" sign was hanging outside when Ruby Wilkinson and her daughter Jean opened it and so they decided to just leave it there. What's in a name, anyway? This friendly, clean-as-a-whistle café has a handwritten menu of daily country-kitchen offerings, all at low, low prices. (All portions are prodigious.) Best of all are the homemade pastries.

240 Decatur Street, French Quarter. 522-5172. Reservations not required. Inexpensive. AE, CB, DC, MC, V.

Light Bites

There actually is no local ordinance here that requires people to stop and eat every ten minutes; it's just more or less customary. Wherever you are you won't be far from food; informal pastry shops and burger joints can be found with no effort whatsoever.

Angelo Brocato's (537 St. Ann Street, French Quarter, 525-9676; 214 N. Carrollton Avenue, Mid-City, 486-0078) was founded when the French Quarter was an Italian neighborhood around the turn of the century. The little, old-fashioned ice-cream shops, with quaint tables and chairs, are operated by the founder's grandchildren. In addition to Italian ices and spumoni, they offer cookies, candies, and wonderful cannoli. (Open daily, inexpensive, no credit cards.)

One of the city's most popular people-watching spots, Café du Monde (800 Decatur Street, French Quarter, 525-4544) has an open-air pavilion with a jumble of tables and chairs. The entire menu is stamped on the napkin holders: *beignets* (three to an order), coffee, *café au lait*, orange juice, and chocolate milk. (Open twenty-four hours every day, inexpensive, no credit cards.)

Coffee and Concierge (334-B Royal Street, French Quarter, 524-5530) is a good place to stop in for a gourmet coffee, tea, pastry, or croissant sandwich when you're antiquing on Royal Street. You can make restaurant and riverboat reservations at the concierge desk. (Open daily, inexpensive, no credit cards.)

Breakfast croissants at Croissant d'Or (617 Ursulines Street, French Quarter, 524-4663) come with almond, raspberry, blueberry, chocolate, and cheese fillings; for lunch there are croissant sandwiches and quiches. You can sit inside or take your plates out into the cheerful courtyard. (Open daily, inexpensive, no credit cards.) The sibling of Croissant d'Or, La Marquise (625 Chartres Street, French Quarter, 524-0420), just off Jackson Square, serves the same croissants and gourmet coffees and has a limited selection of salads. (Open daily, inexpensive, no credit cards.)

When the weather gets hot, everybody heads for Hansen's Sno-Blitz Sweet Shop (4801 Tchoupitoulas Street, 891-9788; hours vary seasonally, so call ahead). Sno-balls are New Orleans' answer to New York's Italian ices—finely shaven ice, flavored with sweet syrups.

Billing itself as a "coffeehouse museum," Kaldi's (941 Decatur Street, French Quarter, 586-8989) has antique coffee machines, sacks of coffee beans, creaky hardwood floors, high ceilings, and a studiously casual clientele that fits into the general scheme of things. Gourmet coffees are served, along with quiches and pastries, and a trio sometimes entertains late at night. (Open twenty-four hours every day, no reservations, inexpensive, no credit cards.)

La Madeleine (547 St. Ann Street, French Quarter, 568-9950) is another hot ticket for breakfast and light lunches. Fresh-baked baguettes, hot soup, fresh-squeezed orange or grapefruit juice, quiche, and croissant sandwiches are served; the display case is filled with brioches, muffins, cookies, and pastries. La Madeleine is a chain, with another location uptown (at 601 Carrollton Avenue) and branches in Texas. (Open daily, no reservations, inexpensive, no credit cards.)

Those people lined up on Decatur across from the Jax Brewery are waiting to get inside Café Maspero (601 Decatur Street, French Quarter, 523-6250) so they can dig into big juicy sandwiches, burgers, and thick-cut fries and knock back the very moderately priced drinks. It doesn't have much in the way of decor but the food is well worth the wait. (Open daily, no reservations, inexpensive, no credit cards.)

Chapter Fourteen
♦♦♦♦♦♦♦♦♦♦♦♦♦♦

Shopping:
Antiques to Zydeco

M OST VISITORS come to the Crescent City to roam Bourbon Street, listen to great jazz, and eat some of the finest food on the planet. But New Orleans is also a great shopping city.

The city's greatest claims to shopping fame are the internationally known antique stores on Royal Street. These long-established shops, many of which are operated now by the third and fourth generations of the founders, are filled with the finest (and most expensive) seventeenth-, eighteenth-, and nineteenth-century European and American furnishings, chandeliers, and *objets d'art*. Royal is also lined with chic art galleries that carry everything from animation art to Renoir.

Although the Quarter is loaded up with sleazy T-shirt shops and ticky-tacky souvenir places, there are treasures to be found even in some of the most suspicious looking bazaars and funky little holes-in-the-wall.

Mardi Gras masks are great souvenirs and are something you're not likely to run across in other North American cities. They come in every imaginable shape, size, and style, from miniature ceramic painted faces and eye masks with plastic plumes to wildly elaborate head-dresses sprouting feathers, sequins, beads, leather, and other froufrous. (Most places will ship, so you don't have to worry about having to wear these on the plane.) Hats, especially Panama hats, are also big sellers. But you can also find some unique handmade hats in several shops, particularly those in the Quarter.

Hardly anyone leaves New Orleans without at least one box of pralines. These candy patties come in many different flavors; you can hardly walk two feet in any direction in the Quarter without coming across a praline purveyor.

Mardi Gras and Jazz Fest posters are also favorite souvenirs. But don't let anyone try to sell you an "official" Mardi Gras poster: There's no such thing. There are some beauties, though, official or no. Jazz records and CDs are other hot tickets to take home. New Orleans jazz musicians are the best in the business, their sounds ranging from traditional jazz to R&B. Cajun music is enormously popular and comes in two flavors: traditional and zydeco, the latter with a faster, zippier rhythm.

Second-line parasols are another only-in-New Orleans item. "Second-liners" are parade followers (the term comes from jazz funerals). Mourners, carrying brightly colored parasols to shade them from the sun, follow the band as it plays slow, heart-rending dirges—"Just a Closer Walk with Thee," for instance—on the way to the cemetery. But once the body has been laid to rest, joyful noises celebrate the release of the deceased's soul—"Oh, Didn't He Ramble!" or an upbeat version of "Closer Walk"—and the former mourners sing and jubilantly wave their parasols. Handmade bisque dolls, too, are utter charmers: antique dolls in crinolines and lace; thumb-sucking babydolls in perambulators; voodoo dolls; African-American, Asian, Creole, and Hispanic dolls; grandmas and grandpas, farmers, and Raggedy Anns and Andys, and Scarlett O'Hara; and tall, sophisticated ladies in frilly picture hats.

There are zillions of books in New Orleans. Cookbooks sell like hot cakes; most of the local restaurateurs have published bestsellers, among them Kevin Graham (Grill Room), Emeril Lagasse (Emeril's and NOLA), Ruby Wilkinson (Miss Ruby and Miss Jean's, also known as the Saddlery), Paul Prudhomme, Alex Patout, *Commander's Palace Cookbook*, and *Brennan's Cookbook*. The city is as rich with history as it is with ingredients; bookshelves groan with books about New Orleans, touching on everything from architecture to Mardi Gras to voodoo.

Most people have a hard time leaving the great New Orleans food. Happily, you can take it with you. Several places have packaged Crescent City specialties—even seafood. If you want to learn how to make some local dishes, you can sign up for a demonstration at the New Orleans School of Cooking in the Jax Brewery (620 Decatur Street, 525-2665) or at the Creole Delicacies Cooking School (Riverwalk, 586-8832). You can even take the sounds of the city home: Your Sound Promenade (282-1932) has produced a ninety-minute cassette tour of the French Quarter, replete with riverboat calliopes, dixieland, and the clip-clop of mules as they pull carriages laden with sightseers. It's for sale in several bookstores around town.

Shopping Districts

The main shopping districts are in the French Quarter and the Central Business District, or CBD. In the Quarter, marvelous shops and bazaars are tucked away in scores of those quaint nineteenth-century creole cottages and town houses. Quarter shopping malls are in the three buildings that make up the Jackson Brewery Complex (620 Decatur

Street, 586-8021): the Jackson Brewery, the adjacent Millhouse, and the Marketplace, a block away on North Peters Street. All three malls are in renovated historic buildings; the Jax Brewery (as most locals call it) and the Millhouse hold scores of specialty shops that are either national chains or locally owned boutiques. The smaller Marketplace has only a handful of retail shops (BookStar and Tower Records/Video among them) and is anchored on the downriver side by the Hard Rock Café, where there is almost always a line waiting to get in.

At the foot of Poydras Street, Riverwalk (1 Poydras Street, CBD, 522-1555) is a lengthy mall that flows upriver with the Mississippi from Spanish Plaza, which is its front yard, to the Convention Center. Riverwalk shops are about a half-and-half mix of local and national stores. Its occupants include Abercrombie & Fitch, Banana Republic, Sharper Image, Victoria's Secret, and the Disney Store as well as New Orleans' Yvonne LaFleur, Louisiana Opal, Street Scenes, DeVille Books, and Mostly Mardi Gras. There are some two hundred specialty stores and eateries. The food court here is as busy and bustling as New York's Fulton Street Market and Boston's Faneuil Hall.

People have been trading in the old French Market since the late seventeenth-century, when there was a trading post on the site. The renovated market, with Café du Monde at the upriver end and the old Farmer's Market downriver, has a host of shops tucked within its arcades and colonnades. Virtually all of the shopkeepers are New Orleans merchants, and they sell everything from candy to quilts. The Farmer's Market, on the same site for well over 160 years, is a string of open-air sheds at which area farmers sell their fresh fruit and produce. Between Barracks and Governor Nicholls Streets, toward the tail end of the market, is a flea market that virtually bursts with jewelry, records, T-shirts, lamps—the usual flea market *junque* (but, this being exotic New Orleans, you can run across some interesting items).

Canal Place (333 Canal Street, CBD, 587-0739) has more than sixty classy shops, among them Saks Fifth Avenue, Gucci, Brooks Brothers, Laura Ashley, and Ann Taylor. There's a food court on the third level as well as three first-run cinemas and the Southern Repertory, a theater group that produces the works of Southern playwrights. The big names at the New Orleans Centre (1400 Poydras Street, CBD, 568-0000) are Lord & Taylor and Macy's; dozens of other shops are chains for the most part (County Seat, Gap, and the like). Magazine Street, which parallels the river (although it does not run right alongside it) all the way from Canal Street to the Audubon Zoo, has a plethora of antique shops, many of them featuring depression glass, secondhand this and that, and jewelry. Mixed in among those shops, however, are some stores with exquisite European antique furnishings. The Warehouse District, a developing pocket in the CBD, has become the city's burgeoning center for contemporary art. Gallery Row on Julia Street is, as the name suggests, a row of galleries featuring abstract and expressionist works by local and national artists.

Riverbend, nestled on the banks of the uptown bend in the Mississippi, has small and charming shops on Dante, Dublin, and especially Hampson Streets. Most of them are locally owned and, cradled in little creole cottages, they make for fun browsing. And, of course, the 'burbs are virtually paved with the concrete shopping malls that can be found in any city.

Louisiana was the first state in the nation to institute Tax-Free Shopping, which applies to international visitors with valid passports and a return ticket and is available in stores that display the LTFS insignia. The program works like this. When making a purchase, show your passport and request a refund voucher for the sales tax.

You'll be charged full price, including sales tax. Keep your sales slip and refund voucher. When you arrive at the airport for your return trip, go to the LTFS refund center and present the sales slip and sales tax refund voucher and your passport and return ticket. Refunds below $100 will be made in cash; those above $100 will be sent in check form to your home address. A handling fee of $5 to $10 is deducted from your refund.

Almost all shops in the French Quarter and the CBD are open daily, though in the Quarter business hours can be quite whimsical. Shops in the malls keep more reliable hours. The Jax Brewery is open Sunday through Thursday from 10:00 to 9:00, Friday and Saturday from 10:00 to 10:00. Canal Place shops are open daily from 10:00 to 6:00 and the mall itself stays open until midnight. New Orleans Centre hours are Monday through Saturday from 10:00 to 8:00, Sunday noon to 6:00. As a very general rule, French Quarter shops open at around 9:30 or 10:00 and close at 5:30 or 6:00. Closing times often depend upon the number of tourists strolling around. The area code for all listings is 504.

Antique Stores

New Orleans contains hundreds of antique stores. The following is a very selective sampling.

♦ *Accent Antiques.* 2855 Magazine, uptown (897-9466). Imported English and European furnishings and prints.

♦ *Blackamoor.* 324 Chartres, French Quarter (523-7786) and 3433 Magazine Street, uptown (897-2711). Antique furniture and porcelain and American art and jewelry.

♦ *Brass Monkey.* 235 Royal, French Quarter (561-0688). Antique walking sticks, small French and English antiques.

♦ *Charbonnet and Charbonnet.* 2929 Magazine, uptown (891-9948). English and Irish country antiques. An in-house cabinet shop for custom-making furnishings using components from razed houses and buildings.

♦ *James H. Cohen & Sons.* 437 Royal, French Quarter (522-3305). Open since 1898. Antique weapons, rare coins, Frederic Remington bronzes, Civil War minié balls, wooden Indians. Marvelous collection of antique miscellanea.

♦ *Curzon Hall.* 3105 Magazine, uptown (899-0078). Dealers in eighteenth- and nineteenth-century furniture. Established in the 1960s in Portobello Road, London.

♦ *Dixon and Dixon.* 237 and 301 Royal, French Quarter (524-0282). Twenty-thousand square feet of seventeenth-, eighteenth-, and nineteenth-century antiques, estate jewelry, antique rugs, European oil paintings.

♦ *French Antique Shop.* 225 Royal, French Quarter (524-9861). Fine eighteenth- and nineteenth-century French furnishings, chandeliers, mirrors, marble mantels, porcelains, bronze statues.

♦ *Diane Genre.* 233 Royal, French Quarter (525-7270). Antique Oriental art, including Japanese wood-block prints, textiles, paintings, lacquer, screens.

♦ *Grand Antiques.* 3125 Magazine, uptown (897-3179). Restored, museum-quality nineteenth-century rosewood grand pianos with ornamental fretwork.

♦ *Jon Antiques.* 4605 Magazine, uptown (899-4482). Eighteenth- and nineteenth-century English and French furniture, mirrors, lamps, porcelains, tea caddies.

♦ *Keil's Antiques.* 325 Royal, French Quarter (522-4552). Since 1899 Keil's has specialized in French and

English antiques, including jewelry, marble mantels, gold leaf mirrors, and chandeliers.

♦ *Gerald D. Katz Antiques.* 505 Royal, French Quarter (524-5050). Collections of Georgian, Victorian, Edwardian, Art Nouveau, Art Deco, and retro jewelry and eighteenth- and nineteenth-century furniture, paintings, *objets d'art.*

♦ *Kohlmaier and Kohlmaier.* 1018 Harmony Street, uptown (895-6394). Rare and unusual antique clocks.

♦ *Lucullus.* 610 Chartres, French Quarter (528-9620). Seventeenth-, eighteenth-, and nineteenth-century culinary antiques including cookware, silverware, china, furnishings, *objets d'art.*

♦ *Manheim Galleries.* 403 Royal, French Quarter (568-1901). Seventeenth- and eighteenth-century English, French, and Continental furniture and fine eighteenth- and nineteenth-century paintings, jade, porcelains.

♦ *Moss Antiques.* 411 Royal, French Quarter (522-3981). Antique jewelry, chandeliers, bric-a-brac.

♦ *19th Century Antiques.* 4838 Magazine, uptown (891-4845). Rare and unusual clocks, cut glass, china, bisques, bric-a-brac, antique watches.

♦ *M. S. Rau.* 630 Royal, French Quarter (523-4662). Royal Street's oldest antique store specializes in American antiques, jewelry, music boxes, silver, porcelain, and glass.

♦ *Royal Antiques.* 307–09 Royal, French Quarter (524-7033). Since 1899 has provided unusual high-quality eighteenth- and nineteenth-century country French and English furnishings, chandeliers, and brass and copper accessories.

◆ *Rothchild's Antiques.* 241 and 321 Royal, French Quarter (523-5816). Antique English and French furniture, chandeliers, marble mantels, silver, porcelain, estate jewelry.

◆ *Henry Stern Antiques.* 329–31 Royal, French Quarter (522-8687). In 1993 Henry Stern, the grand old man of Royal Street, died at the age of ninety-seven. His store is renowned for seventeenth- and eighteenth-century rare Chinese and European porcelains and eighteenth- and nineteenth-century French and English furniture.

◆ *Jack Sutton.* 315 Royal, French Quarter (522-0555). Vintage timepieces, Dresden figurines, carved ivory miniatures.

◆ *Waldhorn's.* 343 Royal, French Quarter (581-6379). Established in 1881. Period eighteenth- and nineteenth-century English furniture, porcelain, silver. Extensive collection of antique American and English jewelry.

Art Galleries

◆ *A Gallery of Fine Photography.* 322 Royal, French Quarter (568-1313). Rare nineteenth- and twentieth-century photographs. Permanent exhibits of Ansel Adams, Diane Arbus, Karsh, Stieglitz, Curtis, Laughlin, and others.

◆ *Ariodante.* 535 Julia Street, Warehouse District (524-3233). Small, chic gallery displaying handcrafted ceramics, jewelry, glass, decorative accessories.

◆ *Bergen Galleries.* 730 Royal, French Quarter (523-7882). Mardi Gras and Jazz Fest posters, limited edition graphics: Erté, Nagel, Hoppe, Nico, Picou.

◆ *Bryant Galleries of New Orleans.* 524 Royal, French Quarter (525-5584). Fine arts, graphics, sculpture, glass. Works by Haitian, European, and American artists.

♦ *Contemporary Arts Center.* 900 Camp Street, Warehouse District (523-1216). Changing exhibits of contemporary art in the CAC's several galleries.

♦ *Fine Arts Gallery of New Orleans.* 614 Canal, CBD (Le Meridien hotel arcade) (522-0691). Museum-quality European and American paintings, sculptures, and watercolors from the seventeenth to the twentieth-centuries. Works by Renoir, Rodin, and Corot are featured.

♦ *Gallerie Simonne Stern.* 518 Julia Street, Warehouse District (529-1113). Fine contemporary paintings, sculpture, photography, and master prints by local, national, and international artists.

♦ *Gasperi Gallery.* 320 Julia Street, Warehouse District (524-9373). Louisiana and Southern folk art, including primitives by Clementine Hunter and works by Andrew Bascle, Jacqueline Bishop, Willie White, and many others.

♦ *Hanson Art Gallery.* 229 Royal, French Quarter (566-0816). Paintings, sculpture, and graphics by Peter Max, Mark Kostabi, Leroy Neiman, Frederick Hart, Erté, and New Orleans' Adrian Deckbar.

♦ *Indigo Nights.* 434 Julia Street, Warehouse District (524-2892). Exquisite antique Louisiana furnishings, carved armoires, handcrafted brass lamps by Guy Wilson, porcelains.

♦ *Rodrigue Gallery.* 721 Royal, French Quarter (581-4244, 800/899-4244). The New Orleans venue for Cajun artist George Rodrigue, world famous for the Blue Dog that appears in his paintings and graphics.

◆ *Arthur Roger Gallery.* 432 Julia Street, Warehouse District (522-1999). Contemporary paintings, sculpture, photographs, works on paper.

◆ *Kurt E. Schon Ltd.* 510 St. Louis Street and 523 Royal Street, French Quarter (524-5462). Eighteenth- and nineteenth-century French and British artworks by impressionists and post-impressionists.

◆ *Virlane Collection.* K & B Plaza, Lee Circle, CBD. Indoor-outdoor exhibit of contemporary art on the plaza and in the lobby of the K & B corporate building. Works by Alexander Calder, Robert Arneson, George Segal, Ida Kohlmeyer, and Masayuki Nagare, among many others.

Books

◆ *Beckham's Bookshop.* 228 Decatur, French Quarter (522-9875). Two floors and shelves jammed with secondhand and rare books. A French Quarter fixture for more than twenty-five years.

◆ *BookStar.* The Marketplace, 414 N. Peters Street, French Quarter (523-6411). Huge two-story bookstore that stocks everything, including books by local and regional authors (Anne Rice, Stephen Ambrose, 1993 Pulitzer Prize–winner Robert Olen Butler), cookbooks, guidebooks: the works.

◆ *DeVille Books and Prints.* One Shell Square, CBD (525-1846) and Riverwalk, CBD (595-8916). Locally owned store selling regional books, guidebooks, cookbooks, maps, posters, prints.

◆ *Faulkner House Books.* 624 Pirate's Alley, French Quarter (524-2940). Located in the building in which William Faulkner wrote his first book, *Soldiers' Pay.* Emphasis on Faulkner and other Southern writers.

♦ *Garden District Book Shop.* 2727 Prytania Street, in the Rink Mall (895-2266). Locally-owned, with an excellent stock of regional books. Conducts searches for hard-to-find books.

♦ *George Herget Books.* 3109 Magazine, uptown (891-5595). A good selection of Louisiana, New Orleans, and Civil War books can be found among the twenty thousand or so old and used books here.

♦ *Librairie.* 823 Chartres, French Quarter (525-4837). A sibling of Beckham's, this too is a big, musty old place with racks, stacks, and shelves of used books.

♦ *Maple Street Book Shop.* 7523 Maple Street, uptown (866-4916); Maple Street Children's Book Shop, 7529 Maple Street, uptown (861-2105). Locally owned, well-stocked bookstores that will conduct searches for hard-to-find books.

Dolls

♦ *Boyer Antiques and Doll Shop.* 241 Chartres, French Quarter (522-4513). Antique dolls, doll restorations, and small antiques.

♦ *Ginja Jar.* 607–611 Royal, French Quarter (523-7643). One of the finest collections of bisque dolls in the city —very high quality, made by local and national artists.

♦ *Hello, Dolly.* 815 Royal, French Quarter (522-9948). An eclectic collection ranging from charming bisque dolls dressed in fine lace and embroidery to tall, sophisticated, dark-skinned Creole dolls to Raggedy Anns and Andys. In the back room, CaSSandra's Enchanted Minikins are some of the most fantastic "soft sculptures" you'll ever see.

♦ *House of Broel.* 1508 St. Charles Avenue, Garden District (522-2220). Regrettably, the dollhouses displayed here are not for sale. There is a truly spectacular collection on three floors of a nineteenth-century Queen Anne mansion.

◆ *Little Toy Shop*. 900 Decatur Street, French Quarter (522-6588). A great collection of bisque dolls, as well as toys of all sorts.

◆ *Oh, Susannah*. 518 St. Peters Street, French Quarter (586-8701). Exquisite collection of old-fashioned dolls, African-American and Asian dolls, babydolls— all dressed in beautifully crafted clothing.

◆ *Le Petit Soldier Shop*. 528 Royal, French Quarter (523-7741). Miniature toy soldiers with fine detailing in uniforms, weapons, and horses.

Hats

◆ *Fleur de Paris*. 712 Royal, French Quarter (525-1899). The displays in the windows of this upmarket ladies' fashion shop are showstoppers; stylish hats are the very latest thing, and clothing can be bought off-the-rack or custom made.

◆ *Yvonne La Fleur*. One Poydras Street, Riverwalk, CBD (522-8222) and 8131 Hampson Street, Riverbend, uptown (866-9666). New Orleans designer Yvonne La Fleur creates smart, very chic women's hats as well as luscious evening and sportswear.

◆ *Little Shop of Fantasy*. 304 Decatur, French Quarter (529-4243). Tracy Keller and Jill Kelly make the delightful cloches, tall top hats and stovepipes, bonnets, and Mad Hatters with oversized crowns.

◆ *Meyer the Hatter*. 120 St. Charles Street (525-1048). In business since 1894, Meyer the Hatter has Panama straws, western Stetsons, fine men's headwear, and even Major League baseball caps.

♦ *Quarter Moon.* 918 Royal, French Quarter (524-3208). The hats made by Tracy Thomson and Ann Marie Popko are decorated with feathers and plumes and all manner of froufrous.

♦ *Rine Chapeaux.* Riverwalk, CBD (523-RINE). This small shop filled with headgear for men and women sells everything from cowboy hats to old-fashioned ladies' bonnets and high-fashion *chapeaux.*

Louisiana Crafts

♦ *Coghlan Galleries.* 710 Toulouse Street, French Quarter (525-8550). Statuary, fountains, and charming garden accessories are displayed in a peaceful courtyard.

♦ *Crafty Louisianian.* 813 Royal, French Quarter (528-3094). Mississippi mud sculptures, Houma Indian moss dolls, Cajun cornstalk dolls, carved wooden figures, palmetto baskets, an assortment of Louisiana handcrafted items.

♦ *Mignon Faget.* Canal Place, CBD (524-2973), and 710 Dublin Street, uptown (865-7361). Mignon Faget finds inspiration in her native New Orleans for the jewelry she makes of 14-karat gold, silver, and bronze-doré. Imaginative earrings, cuff links, tie clasps, and bracelets incorporate miniature renditions of architectural elements, banana leaves, palms, and even sea creatures.

♦ *The Idea Factory.* 838 Chartres, French Quarter (524-5195, 800/524-IDEA). The Bacon family carve these wonderful little wooden paddle-wheelers, alligators, streetcars, roadster convertibles, signs, toy dump trucks and fire engines, miniature working mantel clocks, and scores of other items, from the large to the little.

♦ *Louisiana Living Legends.* Jackson Brewery Millhouse, French Quarter (529-5046). Paintings, woodworks, and other works by Louisianians are displayed and packaged ingredients for Cajun foods are sold in a replica of a Cajun cabin.

♦ *Quarter Moon.* 918 Royal, French Quarter (524-3208). New Orleans motifs, such as tiny Mardi Gras masks, show up in the cuff links, rings, and brooches, all hand made by Michael and Ellis Shallbetter.

♦ *RHINO.* Canal Place, CBD (523-7945). The acronym stands for Right Here In New Orleans, and all of the crafts in this nonprofit shop are made . . . right here. More than seventy artists create the furnishings, paintings, apparel, and decorative items. A very upscale place.

♦ *Street Scenes.* Riverwalk, CBD (595-8865). Master carver Kay Glenn creates scenes of New Orleans and regional culture, including plantations, jazz bands, parades, and riverboats.

♦ *Takis.* 638½ Royal, French Quarter (522-6361). A native of Greece and a horticulturist as well as metal worker, Takis makes lovely museum-quality metal sculptures of flowers.

Louisiana Food-to-Go

♦ *Aunt Sally's Praline Shop.* 810 Decatur, French Quarter (524-5107). You can watch the candy-makers stirring up batches of pralines, and buy boxes to take home or have shipped. The shop has all sorts of souvenir items, including T-shirts, aprons, cookbooks, New Orleans coffee, and *beignet* mix.

♦ *Battistella's Seafood, Inc.* 910 Touro Street, uptown (949-2724, 800/375-2728). Alligator meat, crawfish, soft-shell crabs, shrimp, tuna, and oysters are among the seafoods shipped throughout the country.

♦ *Bayou to Go.* Concourse C, New Orleans International Airport (468-8040). Fresh Louisiana seafoods prepared and wrapped to travel with you on the plane.

♦ *Creole Delicacies.* 523 St. Ann Street, French Quarter (525-9508) and Riverwalk, CBD (523-6425). The specialties are pralines, but there are gift packages of spices, *remoulade* sauce, and hot peppers.

♦ *Gumbo Ya Ya.* 219 Bourbon Street, French Quarter (522-7484). Pralines, fudge, Cajun spices, and homemade sauces are among the take-home items.

♦ *Li'l Fisherman.* 3301 Magazine, uptown (897-9907). A corner fishmarket that prepares fresh Louisiana seafoods to go.

♦ *New Orleans School of Cooking.* 620 Decatur, French Quarter (525-2665). The retail outlet at the cooking school is filled with Louisiana rice, pecans, Cajun spices and sauces, cookbooks, red-beans-and-rice mix, and plenty of other culinary items.

♦ *Old Town Praline Shop.* 627 Royal Street, French Quarter (525-1413). Many Orleanians rate the pralines here the best in town.

Masks

♦ *Crafty Louisianian.* 813 Royal, French Quarter (528-3094). Masks of Mamou, by Acadiana artist Cathy Judice, are the very unusual face masks worn by Cajun horsemen who participate in the Courir de Mardi Gras. The masks are made of painted window screens.

♦ *Hidden Images.* 523 Dumaine Street, French Quarter (524-8730). Elaborate, fanciful feathery masks, full headdresses, and costumes, too.

♦ *Little Shop of Fantasy.* 304 Decatur, French Quarter (529-4243). Michael Stark makes the unusual and exotic masks sold here.

♦ *Mardi Gras Center.* 831 Chartres, French Quarter (524-4384). Most Orleanians make their own Carnival costumes; those that don't get them at this place, which has hundreds of costumes, masks, and other makings for making believe.

♦ *Masks and Make Believe.* Riverwalk, CBD (522-6473). Creations range from small ceramic wall decorations to feathery eye masks to rubber full-face masks of everyone from George Bush to Yoda.

♦ *Mostly Mardi Gras.* Jax Brewery, French Quarter (524-4089). A small but good-quality collection of masks.

♦ *Rumors.* 513 Royal, French Quarter (525-0292). More than a hundred artists create the various masks made of leather, feathers, beads, and sequins; delightful, very fantastical masks here (and at Rumors Too at 319 Royal).

Records and CDs

♦ *GHB Jazz Foundation.* 61 French Market Place, French Quarter (525-1776). A warehouse chock full of traditional jazz, dixieland, and R&B records, CDs, and tapes.

♦ *Louisiana Music Factory.* 225 N. Peters Street, French Quarter (523-1094). Focus is on jazz, Cajun, zydeco, R&B, and other South Louisiana sounds.

♦ *Preservation Hall.* 626 St. Peter Street, French Quarter (523-8939). Only open at night when the bands are playing, it has several bins of records by Preservation Hall veteran recording stars.

◆ *Record Ron's.* 1129 Decatur (524-9444) and 407 Decatur, French Quarter (525-2852). Good selection of music by local and international artists. Country, Cajun, rock, zydeco, national and international artists.

Second-Line Parasols

◆ *Laine's.* 810 Royal, French Quarter (523-2911). Ann Laine often leads the second-lining at the French Market open-air cafés. When she isn't doing that, she's making the parasols that are part and parcel of the parading.

Chapter Fifteen
◆ ◆ ◆ ◆ ◆ ◆ ◆ ◆ ◆ ◆ ◆ ◆

Nightlife

THE SOUTHLAND may have given birth to the blues, but jazz was born right here in New Orleans. Although good musicians have been playing good music in New Orleans since the early 1800s, the man credited with creating the special sounds of jazz is Charles (Buddy) Bolden. An uptown black, born in 1877, Buddy was a natural-born musician. He selected the cornet to play because that's the lead instrument—and Buddy was also a natural-born leader. If even a couple of the legends about Buddy Bolden are true, the man was a musical genius. He could play anything he heard, they say. He could listen to a song, memorize it instrument by instrument, and then improvise on it to make it his own. He listened to the "jubilees" sung in the churches, to the Afro-Caribbean rhythms in Congo Square, to the shouts of the field hands and the cries of the street vendors, and, perhaps most of all, to the brass bands that played all over town. Bolden blended all of those sounds, pushed them through his cornet, and created his own music. Jelly Roll Morton said Buddy was the "blowingest man since Gabriel." (Morton also boasted that he himself "invented" jazz and said New Orleans was the "place where the birth of jazz originated.") By 1900 young Buddy had his own band—and the kind of adulation later known to Valentino, Sinatra, Elvis, and the Beatles.

But though traditional jazz is associated with New Orleans—and properly so—the real down-home New Orleans sound is rhythm and blues. New Orleanians go nuts over native sons the Neville Brothers, who epitomize the New Orleans sound.

Music of all kinds—dixieland, R&B, Cajun, blues, you name it—can be heard almost around the clock on Bourbon Street. The music flooding out of the clubs that line the street flows as freely as the booze. (Actually, it flows a good deal more freely than the booze. Doors are flung wide open, and you can kick back outside and listen for a song. Inside, most imbibing establishments have a two-drink minimum and some require that you take both drinks at once.) A familiar sight on Bourbon is the kids tap-dancing on the streets, hoping for some walking-around money.

Music starts trickling out into the street just after noon, and by early evening the joints are really jumping. Some of the most raucous corners are at St. Louis and Bourbon, where the sounds of Al Hirt, the Dukes of Dixieland, the Cajun Cabin, and Chris Owens roll out and mingle; at Toulouse and Bourbon, where the 544 Club, the Old Opera House (which has nothing whatsoever to do with arias), and the hard-driving clubs in the Inn on Bourbon fight for supremacy; and at St. Peter and Bourbon, where Maison Bourbon, the Cats Meow, the Krazy Korner, and Fritzel's vie for attention. A lot of visitors reel from place to place—and haven't the foggiest where they've been, anyway.

Cheek to jowl with the music clubs are some of the world's tackiest souvenir shops. Your first impression of

Bourbon Street may be that the famous street is not fit for decent folk to walk upon. (Just to get it out of the way: The sleazier topless, bottomless, and female-impersonator places are mostly in the 300 to 500 blocks. "Barkers," who'd be at home on a carnival midway, keep up a steady spiel in attempts to lure revelers inside.) But Bourbon is actually one of the safest streets in town: The city's major tourist attraction is watchfully patrolled. You must, however, beware of pickpockets, some of whom are highly creative.

New Orleans is a twenty-four-hour town. There are no legal closing times, and bars are open even on election day. There are clubs that stay open around the clock, some that close at midnight, and others that don't even open until the witching hour. You can also buy packaged liquor around the clock in whatever grocery store or drugstore is open. (In the Quarter, the Royal Street A & P is an all-nighter; so is the Circle K Food Store at the corner of Dumaine and Royal.)

And speaking of drinks, New Orleans has some doozies. The cocktail is said to have been a New Orleans creation concocted in the mid-nineteenth century by a pharmacist named Antoine Amedée Peychaud. He served his homemade "bitters" to his patrons to cure stomach disorders. Peychaud's bitters came in egg cups, the French name for which was *coquetiers*—a word that the Anglos mangled into "cocktail." As the drink evolved its recipe became Peychaud bitters, Sazerac-da-Forge cognac, and absinthe. Today the only original ingredient is Peychaud bitters; rye whiskey was ultimately substituted for cognac (despite the fact that the cognac gave the drink its name), and Herbsaint—an ersatz absinthe made in New Orleans—is used instead of the illegal absinthe. (The Sazerac is the house drink at the Sazerac bar in the Fairmont Hotel.)

The Hurricane is another libation with a past. Pat

O'Brien's bar served it first (and still makes the best ones). In the 1930s a persuasive salesman sold Pat's partner, Charlie Cantrell, sixty bottles of rum and tossed in gratis some glasses shaped like hurricane lamps. Because the rum wasn't moving, Cantrell eventually added red fruit juice to it, put it in the lamp-shaped glasses, and told the staff to tout it as the new house drink, called the Hurricane. It's sweetly potent and can sneak up on you. The Ramos gin fizz, the Crescent City rendition of a gin fizz, is a mix of gin, orange-flower water, egg whites, and soda. It was first all shook up around the turn of the century.

New Orleans music is not confined to the daytime, nor is it confined to dry land. The Creole Queen (524-0814) does "Dinner on the River and All That Jazz" with a creole buffet and dixieland music. Boarding and buffet begin at 7:00 P.M. and the cruise follows from 8:00 to 10:00 ($39 with the buffet; $18 for the cruise only). Similarly, the Steamboat Natchez (586-8777) does an evening dixieland and dinner cruise. Boarding is at 6:00 P.M. and cruising is from 7:00 to 9:00 ($37.25 with food; $17.50 just for the outing).

Don't forget the jazz brunches. Virtually every restaurant in town does one now, but they originated at Commander's Palace, and many locals think it still has the best ones. Arnaud's does a charmer, and Le Jardin in the Westin Canal Place does a lavish buffet served up with traditional jazz, as does the Blue Room at the Fairmont. Kabby's in the Hilton and Riverview in the Marriott offer spectacular views along with food and music.

Check out the Friday "Lagniappe" tabloid section of the *Times-Picayune* to find out what's doing. The free weekly newspaper *Gambit* also carries calendars and listings of events. The community radio station WWOZ (90.7 FM), which plays and promotes New Orleans music, broadcasts music calendars.

Cover charges range anywhere from $3 to $20, depending upon the importance of the performer or the policy of the place.

Music Clubs

BLUES

♦ *Absinthe House Bar.* 400 Bourbon, French Quarter (525-8108). Gets going around midnight and plays hard-driving blues till dawn's early light.

♦ *Horizons.* Hilton Hotel, 2 Poydras Street, CBD (584-3988). Great river views from the twenty-ninth floor, entertainment by local favorites such as the James Rivers Movement and Marva Wright.

♦ *House of Blues.* 225 Decatur, French Quarter (529-2624). Dan Aykroyd's live-music venue blasted off in early 1994. Local and nationally-known entertainers perform.

♦ *Muddy Waters.* 8301 Oak Street (866-7174), and Benny's Bar, 938 Valence Street (895-9405) are both solid, appropriately funky uptown bastions of blues.

CAJUN

♦ *Cajun Cabin.* 501 Bourbon, French Quarter (529-4256). Live Cajun music and Cajun food nightly, plus 16-ounce souvenir cups of beverages with names like Swamp Water.

♦ *Michaul's Live Cajun Music Restaurant.* 701 Magazine Street, Warehouse District (522-5517). Cajun music, Cajun food, even free Cajun dance lessons on the best dance floor downtown.

♦ *Mulate's.* 201 Julia Street, Warehouse District (522-1492). Offspring of a famous Cajun dance hall in

Breaux Bridge, Louisiana, Mulate's offers good Cajun food, great live Cajun music, and lots of fun.

♦ *Tipitina's.* 501 Napoleon Avenue, uptown (895-8477, concert line 897-3943). The club of choice for most Orleanians, Tip's is an all-purpose sort of place. On Sundays from 4:00 to 9:00 they do a great Cajun *fais-do-do*, a dance that in spirit is not unlike a barn dance or a square dance (with the flavor as Cajun as you can get).

DIXIELAND AND TRADITIONAL JAZZ

♦ *Louis Armstrong Foundation Jazz Club.* Atrium/Le Meridien, 614 Canal Street, CBD (525-6500). The sleek marbled halls of the Meridien provide a pleasant place for listening to rinky-dink piano and dixieland.

♦ *Famous Door.* 339 Bourbon, French Quarter (522-7626). A fixture on Bourbon Street, doing traditional and dixieland since 1934.

♦ *Fritzel's.* 733 Bourbon, French Quarter (561-0432). Jack Maheu and Friends mix it up with dixieland and traditional jazz.

♦ *Jelly Roll's.* 501 Bourbon, French Quarter (568-0501). Al Hirt performs in a big, six-thousand-square-foot room upstairs called Jumbo's. The music here is traditional jazz. Hirt's band starts at 9:30 and the bearded, jumbo-sized trumpeter joins in at 10:00.

♦ *Maison Bourbon.* 641 Bourbon, French Quarter (522-8818). Jazz institutions such as Wallace Davenport, Tommy Yetta, and Steve Slocum perform in this little corner joint.

♦ *Maxwell's.* 615 Toulouse, French Quarter (523-4207). New Orleans District Attorney Harry Connick, Sr.,

Judy England, Jimmy Maxwell and his Orchestra, and Banu Gibson and New Orleans Hot Jazz liven things up here. Shows are nightly at 9:00, 10:00, and 11:00. Occasionally Harry Jr. will stop in to sing along with pop, but don't make a special trip: It's a rarity.

◆ *Palm Court Jazz Cafe.* 1204 Decatur, French Quarter (525-0200). A real treat. Feast on jambalaya, steak and mushroom pie, and red beans and rice while you listen to marvelous music. Most nights there's lively second-lining, and you might get swept up in it whether you intended to or not. A very fun place.

◆ *Pete Fountain's Club.* Hilton Hotel, 2 Poydras Street, CBD (523-4374). An all-time great clarinetist, native son, and ubiquitous ambassador for New Orleans, Pete plays at 10:15 Tuesday, Wednesday, Friday, and Saturday nights. (The club opens Tuesday through Saturday at 10:00 P.M.) Pete tours a lot, so it's best to check if he's in town. Reservations required.

◆ *Preservation Hall.* 726 St. Peter Street, French Quarter (night 523-8939, day 522-2841). The city's most famous music parlor is also among the grungiest, but the musicians are the all-time greats of the traditional jazz genre: the Humphrey brothers, Willie and Percy, Kid Sheik, the Olympia Jazz Band. Most of them hover around ninety but there are younger up-and-comers who will keep the torch burning.

ROCK

◆ *Hard Rock Café.* 440 N. Peters Street, French Quarter (529-5617). Iconography at the New Orleans piece of the Rock include Elton John's shoes, Fats Domino's piano top (lying above the guitar-shaped bar), and the standing bass used by the Stones to record "Ruby Tuesday."

◆ *Jimmy's Club.* 8200 Willow Street, uptown (861-8200). The college crowd flocks in to hear local and national bands knock out hard rock.

Mixed Bag

◆ *Jimmy Buffett's Margaritaville.* 1104 Decatur, French Quarter (592-2565). Local entertainers take to the stage around 10:30 P.M. When Buffett's in town, he takes the stand. (Don't miss the conch fritters, "cheeseburger in paradise," and Key lime pie.)

◆ *O'Flaherty's Irish Channel.* 508 Toulouse, French Quarter (529-1317). The Irish O'Flaherty brothers, Danny and Patrick, run a tavern *cum* Celtic educational center. The Celtic Folk entertain nightly (when Tommy Makem or the Clancy Brothers are in town, this is where they appear), and Gaelic language and dance lessons are offered.

◆ *Pat O'Brien's.* 718 St. Peter Street, French Quarter (525-4823). One of the world's most renowned bars, Pat's has been around since the early 1930s. New Orleans may have given birth to jazz, but Pat's was the father of the Hurricane; the mixologists here still make them better than anybody else. There are three bars here, the rowdiest of which is a piano bar with tiny tables, two piano-playing ladies, and an enthusiastic crowd that loves to holler along. There's also a lovely courtyard, one of the prettiest in town, with a glorious illuminated fountain that spouts both fire and water.

◆ *Snug Harbor.* 626 Frenchmen Street, Faubourg Marigny (949-0696). A sizzling spot that features local greats such as Ellis Marsalis (father of Wynton and Branford) and Charmaine Neville. The restaurant serves pretty good burgers and fries.

♦ *Tricou House.* 711 Bourbon, French Quarter (525-8379). Seafood and jazz are served up in a historic nineteenth-century house.

♦ *The Tropical Isle* (738 Toulouse, 525-1689) and Molly's (732 Toulouse, 568-1915), both in the French Quarter, never close, and the music is live and varied. Sandwiched between them is the Dungeon. The Dungeon, which has no discernible street address and no phone, is one of those underground places about which word gets around. It's been there for ages, and every celebrity who comes to town eventually winds up there. A bar and minuscule disco with a DJ maestro, it opens around midnight and closes sometime the next morning. Locals love it.

Dance Clubs

♦ *City Lights.* 310 Howard Avenue, Warehouse District (568-1700). Young Warehouse District professionals gather in the chic City Lights to dance to DJ music from the fifties through the nineties. Thursday night is ladies' night; live music happens on Friday nights after 9:00. A strict dress code prohibits T-shirts, jeans, shorts, or tennis shoes.

♦ *Hog's Breath Saloon and Café.* 339 Chartres, French Quarter (522-1736). Upstairs there's a dance floor and DJ (and live music occasionally), downstairs a café with good cheeseburgers. Sunday afternoons frequently see all-you-can-eat crawfish to the tune of live country music.

♦ *Lucky Pierre's World Beat.* 735 Bourbon, French Quarter (523-5842). A happening place with a piano bar, dance club, custom-made video wall, pool table, and game room. World music is interspersed with Top 40 tunes. The crowd is young.

♦ *Maple Leaf Bar.* 8316 Oak Street, uptown (866-9359). This is an uptown bar with a tiny dance floor, a friendly crowd, and a mixed bag of music. You can almost bank on Cajun music Thursday nights and zydeco on Fridays. A great place.

♦ *Mid-City Bowling Lanes and Sports Palace.* 4133 S. Carrollton Avenue, uptown (482-3133). This is New Orleans and anything goes. This is indeed a bowling alley where people bowl, but Friday is Rock 'n' Bowl night, with live music, dancing, bowling, and great good fun.

♦ *Mudbugs.* 2024 Belle Chase Highway, Gretna, on the West Bank (392-0202). Mudbugs claims it's the world's biggest honky-tonk: Who's to argue? The music is mostly country and there's sixty-five-hundred square feet of floor space for line dancing. Top-name entertainers who appear here include Willie Nelson and Garth Brooks.

Revues

♦ *The Mint.* 504 Esplanade Avenue, Faubourg Marigny (525-2000). Satirical, outrageously funny shows draw a mix of gays and straights—all of whom get a large charge out of the skits.

♦ *Chris Owens.* 500 Bourbon, French Quarter (523-6400). Virtually a legend on Bourbon, Chris Owens does a glitzy, fast-paced Vegas-style show with lots of costume changes and a backup trio. She performs six nights a week (no Sundays) with shows at 10:00 and midnight. There's a small floor for dancing between sets.

Bars

♦ *Café Lafitte in Exile.* 901 Bourbon, French Quarter (522-8377). This has for years been a popular gay bar; it's still going strong.

♦ *Harry's Place.* 900 Chartres, French Quarter (524-7052). A neighborhood hole-in-the-wall that closes only for a few hours on Ash Wednesday to clean up the mess. The decor consists of a long wooden bar, barstools, a cigarette machine, and a big barber chair next to the TV set.

♦ *Lafitte's Blacksmith Shop.* 941 Bourbon, French Quarter (523-0066). Legend continues to have it that Jean and Pierre Lafitte had a blacksmith shop in this little house as a front for their illegal slave-trading and smuggling activities. The tattered old cottage dates from around 1772, and it looks its age. It's been a favorite neighborhood watering hole for ages and ages.

♦ *Napoleon House.* 500 Chartres, French Quarter (524-9752). A landmark as well as a favorite local bar, especially for artists and writers, the Napoleon House is so named because a group of the Little Corporal's admirers meant to rescue him from exile and bring him here to live. The plan fizzled, but the bar is *the* hanging-out place.

♦ *Old Absinthe House.* 240 Bourbon, French Quarter (523-3181). This old bar has been on Bourbon since the early nineteenth-century—chances are that in the early days there were no football helmets dangling over the bar. The walls are papered from floor to ceiling with business cards from all over the world.

♦ *Que Sera.* 3636 St. Charles Avenue (897-2598). On Wednesday evenings the big crowds around here aren't gathered for a block party: They're here for the weekly three-for-one drinks. There's a pleasant verandah where you can sit and watch the streetcar rumble up and down the avenue.

♦ *Sazerac Bar.* Fairmont Hotel, University Place, CBD (529-7111). A favorite meeting place for the city's movers and shakers, the handsome Sazerac has an African walnut bar and colorful murals of New Orleans scenes painted by Paul Ninas. The bar played a role in *The Pelican Brief* and in *Blaze*, in which Paul Newman portrayed Governor Earl Long (the Sazerac was a favored hangout for both Huey and Earl Long).

Coffeehouses

♦ *Café Brazil.* 2100 Chartres, French Quarter. This place is so bohemian it doesn't even have a phone—except for the pay phone that nobody ever answers. Nonetheless, it's dear to the hearts of many an Orleanian for its casual, kick-back style and for the poetry readings and musical potluck.

♦ *Kaldi's.* 941 Decatur, French Quarter (586-8989). This very laid back sixties-style space serves up gourmet coffees, pastries, and quiches and a mixed bag of gospel, jazz, and blues. Open twenty-four hours.

♦ *True Brew.* 200 Julia Street, Warehouse District (524-8441). This casual coffeehouse often presents local actors in acclaimed one-acts.

Theater, Music, and Opera

Truth to tell, dixieland, R&B, traditional jazz, and gutbucket dominate the music scene in the city. But for those who seek higher-brow entertainment, they, too, can find diversions.

The New Orleans City Ballet (522-0996) and the New Orleans Opera (529-2278) perform at the Theatre of the Performing Arts in Armstrong Park (801 N. Rampart Street, 565-7470). The Louisiana Philharmonic Orchestra (523-6530) plays classics and pops concerts in the Orpheum Theatre (129 University Place, 524-3285). The New Orleans Pops (525-7677) performs at various venues throughout the city.

Broadway touring shows and top-name talent perform at the Saenger Performing Arts Center (143 N. Rampart Street, 524-2490). National headliners also appear at the Kiefer UNO Lakefront Arena (6801 Franklin Avenue, 286-7222). The Louisiana Superdome (1500 Poydras Street, CBD, 587-3800) hosts everything from Ringling Bros. to the Rolling Stones and Paul McCartney.

- *Contemporary Arts Center.* 900 Camp Street (523-1216; box office 528-3800). The avant-garde and the outrageous are among the offerings in the CAC's two theaters.

- *Le Petit Theatre du Vieux Carré.* 616 St. Peter Street, French Quarter (522-2081, 522-9958). The country's oldest continuously operated community theater presents a season of plays on the main stage beginning in September and running through June. The Children's Corner also does productions aimed at the little ones.

- *Southern Repertory Theater.* Canal Place, CBD (861-8163). The works of Southern playwrights are the focus. During the summer the rep presents a New Playwrights series.

- *Theatre Marigny.* 616 Frenchmen Street (944-2653). This pocket-sized theater also presents the works of unknown playwrights as well as those of established ones.

Chapter Sixteen
♦♦♦♦♦♦♦♦♦♦♦♦♦

Crescent City Logistics

NEW ORLEANS International Airport, also called Moisant Field, is about fifteen miles west of the city in the town of Kenner. The drive into town takes about twenty to thirty minutes, depending upon traffic. The taxi fare is set at $21 for one or two passengers and $8 for each additional passenger. The cab stand is just outside the baggage claim area.

The Airport Shuttle, which makes pickups just outside the baggage claim area, drops off passengers at all of the hotels and guesthouses. One-way fare is $10. The duration of the trip depends upon whether your hotel is first or last on the route. To reserve space for the return trip, call 522-3500. (The telephone area code for all listings is 504. A public bus, operated by Louisiana Transit (737-9611), runs between the airport and Elk Place in the CBD. The cost is only $1.10, but because the bus makes regular stops the trip can take up to an hour.

All of the major car rental agencies have outlets at the airport. I-10 is the east-west artery through town; I-12 is an east-west route on the North Shore of Lake Pontchartrain. North-south I-55 connects with I-10 west of the city; I-59, which also runs north-south, connects with I-12 northeast of New Orleans.

If you plan to drive in the city, there are things you should bear in mind, not the least of which is that New Orleanians drive like bats out of the Bad Place. Only a few hotels offer free parking; in most the daily charge ranges from about $4 to $12. Driving in the French Quarter—especially during Mardi Gras or other special events—is a nightmare, and street parking is another tale from the crypt. Parking signs in the Quarter are indecipherable, and New Orleans tow-truck drivers move faster than the speed of light—their joy in tackling their tasks is the envy of all other working stiffs. If your car is towed away, the Tow Pound is at 400 North Claiborne Avenue (565-7450). The ticket can be upwards of $100—exclusive of a little something to soothe your nerves.

Unlike parking signs, street signs in the Quarter are easy to read. In most other sections of the city, however, you almost have to get out of your car to read them—and that's if you have 20/20 vision. The French Quarter has secured parking garages in the Maison Blanche Building (entrance on Dauphine Street between Canal and Iberville Streets), Westminster Parking at 721 Iberville, and Dixie Parking at 911 Iberville. There are large open lots at the Jax Brewery on Decatur Street and behind the French Market from Dumaine to Toulouse Streets.

The Union Passenger Terminal at 1001 Loyola Avenue in the CBD serves as both train and bus station for New Orleans. Amtrak trains (800/872-7245) connect New Orleans with Florida, California, Chicago, New York, and points in between. Greyhound (800/231-2222) provides regular service between New Orleans and cities small and large.

The Regional Transit Authority (RTA) operates the city's vast public transit system. Fare for all buses and streetcars, except the Riverfront Streetcar, is one dollar (exact change) and 10 cents for transfers. Fare for the Riverfront Streetcar, which connects French Quarter destinations between Esplanade Avenue and Julia Street, is $1.25 (exact change). The RTA staffs a twenty-four-hour information line (569-2700).

VisiTour passes are good buys and offer unlimited travel on buses and streetcars. One-day passes cost $4 and three-day passes are $8. They're sold in hotels and in shopping malls.

The St. Charles Streetcar—a National Historic Landmark—is the oldest continuously operating street railway system in the world. It began in 1835 as a railroad that connected Canal Street with the city of Carrollton, which was long ago annexed by the city. (New Orleanians never say "trolley"—no one knows quite why.) The streetcar rumbles and clangs all the way from Canal up St. Charles to South Carrollton Avenue, which is as far as it can rumble without clanging into the Mississippi. It turns on South Carrollton and stops at the end of the line, Palmer Park. A round-trip ride on the streetcar, about ninety minutes, gives you a good overview of St. Charles Avenue, the Garden District, and the uptown and university sections. It'll cost you an additional dollar to get back to Canal. (This outing is not advisable weekday mornings between 8:00 and 9:30 or afternoons between about 2:30 and 5:30, when schoolchildren and commuters cram the cars.)

A ferry—free to pedestrians—runs between the foot of Canal across the Mississippi to Algiers, a residential community on the West Bank. Cars taking the trip to Algiers also ride for free, but the fare for the return to Canal is one dollar per vehicle. The ferry operates every half hour from 5:30 A.M. until 9:30 P.M. Bear in mind that the 9:30 crossing to Algiers is the last of the day; the ferry doesn't return to Canal Street, and pedestrians will be hard pressed indeed to find a way back to the East Bank. Don't risk it.

Taxi fares start at $1.70 and cost one dollar for each additional mile, plus 50 cents for each additional person (that is, two people climbing into a cab automatically jack the drop up to $2.20). Cabs charge $3 per person for special events—say, to go from the Quarter to the Fair Grounds during Jazz Fest. Cabs are easy to flag down in the Quarter and the CBD but they don't generally cruise outside the downtown tourist areas. If you go for a jaunt to other environs, plan to call a cab to pick you up and take you back to your hotel.

The most reliable cab company in the city is United Cabs (522-9771, 800/323-3303). If you want a United cab to pick you up when you arrive at the airport, call the toll-free number and give your name, the date, and your time of arrival, airline, and flight number. Most United cabbies take major credit cards, but make sure you request a cab that accepts them.

Tourist Information

For help in planning your trip, write first to the Greater New Orleans Tourist and Convention Commission (1520 Sugar Bowl Drive, New Orleans 70112, 504/566-5011), which will provide you with all sorts of free information.

When you arrive, visit the New Orleans Welcome Center (566-5031), which shares space with the Louisiana Office of Tourism, on Jackson Square (529 St. Ann Street). Free maps, brochures, self-guided walking and driving tours, and plenty of good advice are yours for the asking. Be sure to pick up the map that shows the main tourist routes of the streetcars and buses.

The Folklife Center of the Jean Lafitte National Historical Park Service (916–18 N. Peters Street, French Market, 589-2636) also has a wealth of useful information.

The French Quarter is under the auspices of the Park Service, as is the Chalmette Unit downriver, where the Battle of New Orleans was fought in 1815, and the Barataria Unit, where there are swamps and 'gators to see and canoes to rent. The Folklife Center also has excellent exhibits on Louisiana culture and ecology.

Guide Services

Park Rangers (589-2636) do free daily walking tours of the French Quarter, Faubourg Marigny, and the Garden District. The ninety-minute tours begin at the Folklife Center and are conducted rain or shine. The *Friends of the Cabildo* (523-3939) also conducts walking tours of the Quarter; the $10 cost ($5 for ages thirteen to twenty and for seniors) covers admission to two of the Louisiana State Museum properties. Tours start at the Museum Store on Jackson Square (523 St. Ann Street) Tuesday through Sunday at 10:00 A.M. and 1:30 P.M. and Monday at 1:30. *Save our Cemeteries* (588-9357) does ninety-minute walking tours of St. Louis Cemetery No. 1, the city's oldest extant cemetery. The cost is $8, and the group meets Sunday mornings at 10:00 at the Royal Blend Coffee Shop (623 Royal Street). *Heritage Tours* (949-9805) offers a variety of tours and walks that focus on the city's rich literary history. *Classic Tours* (899-1862) take in the city's art, architecture, antiques, and history.

If you'd rather do your sightseeing on wheels, contact Gray Line (587-0861), New Orleans Tours (592-0560), or Tours by Isabelle (367-3963). All three companies make hotel pickups and offer two- or three-hour city tours and half- or full-day plantation country and swamp tours. Gray Line's two-hour city tour costs $17.50 ($8.50 for children); New Orleans Tours' two-hour city tour costs $17 ($9 for children); and Tours by Isabelle does a three-hour city tour for $25. Both Gray Line and New

Orleans Tours do combination bus tours and riverboat
cruises for $29 ($14.25 for children) and $28 ($14 for
children), respectively. New Orleans Tours also does a
$40 "Pete Fountain's Jazz Extravaganza" and a $38
nightlife tour. Dr. Paul Wagner, a wetland ecologist,
conducts flatboat tours of Honey Island Swamp, one of
the country's least altered wetlands. In addition to pointing out alligators, blue herons, beavers, and other critters,
he'll tell you about the swamp monster said to inhabit
these parts. Tours are $20 ($10 for children)—$40 ($20
for children) with hotel pickup (242-5877).

Other Services

♦ *Automobile repairs*—American Automobile Association, 3445 Causeway Boulevard, Metairie (838-7500)
  and CBD Chevron Services, 447 N. Rampart Street
  (568-1177)

♦ *Barber*—Canal Place Barber Shop, 1 Canal Place (522-
  4147)

♦ *Beauty salon*—Lulu Buras, Canal Place (523-5858)

♦ *Camera repairs*—AAA Camera Repair, 1631 St.
  Charles Avenue (593-9690)

♦ *Dry Cleaning, laundry, tailoring*—One-Hour Martin-
  izing, 4842 Perrier (895-3046)

♦ *Fax and photocopying*—Kinko's, 762 St. Charles Avenue (525-3278); open twenty-four hours)

♦ *Limousine service*—London Livery, 3037 Royal Street
  (944-1984)

♦ *Medical emergency*—Tulane Medical Center, 1415 Tu-
  lane Avenue (588-5711); Children's Hospital, 200
  Henry Clay Avenue (899-9511); Touro Infirmary, 1401
  Foucher Street (897-8250)

+ *Messenger*—United Cabs (522-9771)

+ *National-international courier*—Federal Express (800/238-5355); Airborne (800/999-2481); DHL (800/225-5345)

+ *Optical*—Vision Plaza, New Orleans Centre, 1400 Poydras Street (586-8904)

+ *Pharmacy*—K & B, 3401 St. Charles Avenue (895-0344); Walgreen's, 900 Canal Street (523-7201); twenty-four-hour Walgreen's stores: 3311 Canal Street (822-8073) and 3057 Gentilly Boulevard (282-2621)

+ *Police and other emergencies*—call 911

+ *Post office*—main post office, 701 Loyola Avenue (589-1111); Vieux Carré station, 1022 Iberville Street (524-0072).

+ *Radio news*—WWL Radio, 870 AM.

+ *Secretarial services*—Executive Business Center, Royal Sonesta Hotel, 300 Bourbon Street (586-0586) and Kelly Temporary Services, 1515 Poydras Street (529-1451)

+ *Shoe repairs*—Tip-Top Shoe Repairs, 1027 Iberville Street (522-5740) and 902 Poydras Street (522-8870)

+ *Travel accessories*—Rapp's Luggage and Gifts, 604 Canal Street (568-1953) and New Orleans Centre, 1400 Poydras Street (566-0700)

+ *Western Union*—Royal Street A & P, 701 Royal Street (523-1353); 334 Carondelet Street (529-5971)

Climate and Clothing

Summers in New Orleans last about nine months. By mid-March the azaleas are in bloom, and by early May things have begun to sizzle. June, July, and August are the hottest months, when the temperature soars into the high 90s and stays there. During those months it rains at least a little almost every day. Whatever the time of year, bring an umbrella and sunglasses; it is not uncommon to have a downpour while the sun is shining brightly.

Winters are devilishly unpredictable. December temperatures can be in the 80s—the average is around 60 degrees—or a shivery 45 degrees. Laugh if you will, but if you're here when it's in the mid-40s or even around 50 you'll see that the high humidity and winds off the river can make moderate-sounding temperatures really vicious. The coldest months are usually January and February. Again, the average for those months is 40-ish, but the dampness goes right through you.

Daytime dress in New Orleans is casual, particularly in the French Quarter, where short shorts, halters, tank tops, and flip-flops are in style year round. In such attire, you're likely to feel overdressed when you encounter French Quarter characters who routinely amble about in stark-white clown makeup, baggy pants, and red fright wigs.

Although cotton doesn't pack as well as synthetics, it is much cooler. In the summer, women should pack light-weight dresses for dining out; sundresses are fine for most places, but air-conditioning goes at full blast everywhere and you might yearn for something around your shoulders. Men should pack lightweight slacks and jackets; restaurant dress codes are somewhat more lax in the summer, but many insist upon jackets. Bring the most casual clothing you have for daytime sightseeing and be sure to bring comfortable walking shoes—New Orleans sidewalks are old, cracked, and in some cases, crumbling. You'll also want topsiders or such for riverboat outings.

Go for the layered look in winter. The most practical thing you can bring is an all-weather coat with a zip-out lining. Bring casual gear for daytime wear; winter evening wear is more formal than in the summer, but you'll have no need for long gowns or tuxes.

Index